GREAT FISHING IN
LAKE ONTARIO
& TRIBUTARIES

THE GOOD FISHING IN NEW YORK SERIES

GOOD FISHING CLOSE TO NEW YORK CITY
GREAT FISHING IN LAKE ONTARIO AND TRIBUTARIES
GOOD FISHING IN THE CATSKILLS

GREAT FISHING IN LAKE ONTARIO & TRIBUTARIES

RICH GIESSUEBEL

NORTHEAST SPORTSMAN'S PRESS
TARRYTOWN, NEW YORK

STACKPOLE BOOKS
HARRISBURG, PENNSYLVANIA

Library of Congress Cataloging-in-Publication Data

Giessuebel, Rich.
    Great fishing in Lake Ontario & tributaries.

    (The Good fishing in New York series)
    1. Fishing — Ontario, Lake, Watershed (N.Y. and Ont.) —
Guide-books.   I. Title.   II. Series.
SH529.G54   1987   799.1'1'097479   87-11023
ISBN 0-942990-08-0
ISBN 0-942990-09-9 (soft)
ISBN 0-942990-16-1 (soft, revised)

All photography by the author except: Ron Jacobsen
(pp. 49, 115,169, 176, 191,193, 217); Andy Gennaro
(pp. 2, 136); Robert Kennedy (p. 170); Dave Mann (p. 104);
and Alice Vera (p. 46).

Published by Stackpole Books and
Northeast Sportsman's Press
Distributed by Stackpole Books
Cameron & Kelker Streets
P.O. Box 1831
Harrisburg, Pennsylvania 17105

Printed in the United States of America

10-9-8-7-6-5-4-3

WARNING!

The New York State Department Of Health warns that most fish in Lake Ontario and its tributaries have elevated levels of certain contaminants. See the summary of these advisories in Chapter 2. Also contact the New York State Department Of Environmental Conservation for current advisories on this situation.

ACKNOWLEDGEMENTS

The author wishes to acknowledge the following individuals, for their companionship and for their assistance in making this book as current, accurate and complete as possible:

Mike Kersey, Ron Jacobsen, Andy Gennaro, Floyd Moore, Roosevelt Hughes, Joe Rosa, Robert Kennedy, Ray Finny, Russ Wilson, the late Howard Cavillero, Capt. Ron Clark, Jack Baker, Deborah Somers, Chuck Krupke, Capt. Rick Rockefeller, Capt. Richard Streich, Walt Wiedmont, Capt. Paul Lewandowski, Capt. Charles DeNoto, Capt. Ed Dorscheid, Capt. John Kowalczyk, George R. Seeley, Jr., Capt. Paul Petrie, Capt. Carl Rathke, George Metzler, Tony Gugino, Dave Mann, John Riley and J.D.

And special thanks to Ernie Schleusener and the Mann's Tackle Company, and to *The Fisherman* magazine for first inspiring me to look into the fishing potential of this region.

TABLE OF CONTENTS

ILLUSTRATIONS

IMPORTANT NOTES ON THE TEXT

A number of geographical terms are used in this book to describe where to fish in Lake Ontario. Here are the definitions of these terms *as we use them in this book*. All of these are depicted on the accompanying map. We also here define a few other terms and abbreviations used in the book.

Southern tier — Lake Ontario locations on the U.S.A. side between Fort Niagara and Oswego.
Northern tier — Lake Ontario locations on the U.S.A. side northeast of Oswego.
Bay — a "dent" in the Lake Ontario shoreline, usually somewhat calmer and more protected than the main lake. Bays will vary greatly in size, and some may be fed by tributary streams.

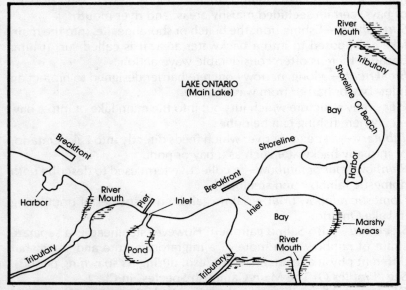

► *This is a representation only, not an actual area of Lake Ontario.*

Harbor — body of water offering protection and calmer waters for boats and boaters. Often located within the most protected portion of a bay.

Pond — small body of water, somewhat detached from the main lake but connected to it usually by a simple outlet.

Inlet — an opening, often quite narrow, between an inland body of water (such as a bay or a pond) and the main lake.

River mouth — the downstream end of a Lake Ontario tributary where it widens and empties into a bay or pond or the main lake. River mouths are often braced by considerable wetlands which serve as nursery areas for many different types of immature fish.

Shore — a collective term used to describe *any* place where an angler stands on shore (or wades) to fish Lake Ontario or any of its backwaters.

Shoreline or beach — used interchangeably. Describes any location (sand, rock, pier, etc.) where an angler fishes directly into the main lake.

Backwater — a collective term used to describe any protected, inland water on Lake Ontario, such as ponds, certain bays or parts of bays, certain secluded marshy areas, and river mouths.

Surf fishing — fishing from the beach or shoreline, i.e. into the main lake as opposed to into a backwater area. It is called surf fishing because there is often considerable wave action.

Breakfront — a long, narrow concrete barrier designed to protect an inlet, bay or harbor from wave action.

Pier — any structure which juts out into the main lake or into a bay, etc., where fishing can be done.

Tributary — a stream or river which feeds directly into Lake Ontario, or into any backwater such as a bay or pond.

Rainbow trout or rainbow — a collective term used to describe *both* domestic rainbow and steelhead.

Domestic rainbow trout — Salmo gairdneri, a species of trout living in Lake Ontario.

Steelhead — also Salmo gairdneri. However steelhead is a separate strain of rainbow with more of a migratory nature and somewhat different physical characteristics (esp. during its spawning period). See "Profiles Of The Main Gamefish Species" in Ch. 1.

DEC — an abbreviation for the New York State Department Of Environmental Conservation.

INTRODUCTION

Many are calling it the greatest freshwater fishing in the world! One of the world's "greatest" lakes, Lake Ontario, is seeing an unprecedented explosion of its appeal as a mecca for sportfishermen. Seventeen years of undaunted efforts by New York State and other agencies have paid off with truly fabulous fishing for a host of different species. Not only have some of the native fish been restored, but now anglers can try for such west coast favorites as the giant chinook and coho salmon.

Unlike Alaska and many other remote or far northern places, fish are caught with regularity here during every month of the year. Also unlike Alaska, New York State's Lake Ontario offers a two temperature fishery. Those interested in the cold water species can catch trout and salmon, while those interested in warm water sport can garner large and smallmouth bass, walleye, muskellunge, perch, and northern pike in season. With many of these species growing to lunker proportions, Lake Ontario is seeing a fishing boom unparalleled in the history of American sportfishing.

If you have ever wanted to fish in Alaska, but have found the cost prohibitive, Lake Ontario may be for you. Here the fishing is second to none, fine hotels and restaurants are everywhere, airports and major cities are spread out over a 180 mile shoreline, tackle shops, guides, and everything you may require are all within the range of any modest budget.

This book is the first complete guide to one of North America's greatest freshwater fisheries: New York State's Lake Ontario and its tributaries. Knowing the varieties of fish that inhabit these waters, where to catch them, when to catch them, and how to catch them will prepare you for the fishing experience of a lifetime. Good fishing and don't let that world record get away!

ABOUT THE GOOD FISHING IN NEW YORK SERIES

What state in the union has 4,000 lakes over 6.4 acres in size? Or 3,400,000 total acres of lakes? Or 70,000 miles of rivers, 15,000 of these supporting trout?

And what state has 1,200,000 acres of coastal water? Or 1,850 miles of coastline?

The answer is, only New York State has all of this in combination.

We believe, in fact, that New York State offers the *best* fishing of any state in the country, and it is oh so wonderfully close to so many people.

But let's get a little more specific. Where else can you find together all this: Hundreds of miles of shoreline on two Great Lakes; over a hundred more miles of shoreline on the sixth largest lake in the country (Lake Champlain); a magnificent and biologically rich great estuary (the Hudson); not one but *two* major mountain ranges (the Catskills and the Adirondacks); a virtual cornucopia of coastal waters, including bays, inlets, cuts, islands, points, and immense Long Island Sound; a beautiful heartland laced with huge, clean, deep, glacially-formed lakes (the one and only Finger Lakes Region); America's "Most Beautiful Lake" (Lake George); intriguing tidal rivers where sea-run trout abound; tens of thousands of acres of clean and undeveloped watershed reservoirs; plus many other surprises?

The answer is, of course, only in New York State.

With the amazing amount of fishing available in the Empire State, a series of five, comprehensive guidebooks was not only justified but, we felt, long overdue. We believe each book in this series to be of the highest quality, both in terms of editorial content and graphic support. Each contributing author is a true expert on his/her particular subject. In most cases, the authors live in the area they have written about and have ten, twenty or more years of actual fishing experiences on the waters they discuss. There are no armchair experts connected with this series of books at all.

The accurate text is supported by dozens of clean, usable maps, plus dozens more illustrations, graphs, sidebars, charts and more. These are true guidebooks, and the 8¼'' by 5½'' size lets them go easily along in glove compartment or tackle bag.

I hope you will look for each of the five volumes that will eventually constitute the GOOD FISHING IN NEW YORK SERIES (the map on the back cover of each book shows the geographical breakdown of the series). And I hope you will actually use these books, and take them with you, to help you explore the best fishing that America has to offer — right here in beautiful New York State.

Jim Capossela
Creator of the GOOD FISHING IN NEW YORK SERIES

To my constant companions, wife Judy
and sons John and Steven, who have endured
much with my countless excursions to the Great Lakes.

GETTING READY FOR THE FISHING TRIP OF YOUR LIFE

PART I

GENERAL DESCRIPTION OF THE LAKE

"and farther below, Lake Ontario, takes in what Lake Erie can send her. And the iron boats go, as the mariners all know, with the Gales of November remembered!"

From "The Wreck of the Edmund Fitzgerald"

Although Lake Ontario is the smallest of the five great lakes, it is still an enormous body of water and the 15th largest lake in the world. In it, the State of Rhode Island could be placed some five times. To make another comparison, it is 193 miles long and 53 miles wide at its widest point . . . the approximate dimensions of the State of New Jersey. Lake Ontario separates the United States from Canada along the northern New York State border.

The lake sits 245 feet above sea level, and has a maximum depth of 802 feet. It is 480 miles around the lake, which encompasses 7,520 square miles. Lake Ontario never freezes over in the winter and is a major shipping thoroughfare for liners coming in from the St. Lawrence Seaway to inland ports and vice versa.

ORIGINS

Scientists peg the beginning of the Great Lakes within the past one million years or so. Created during the Ice Ages or Pleistocene Epoch, Lake Ontario and the others were once thought to be simple streams running through simple countrysides. But then, things began to change. Ice sheets, some five miles thick, began moving down along their courses on as many as five different occasions. Slowly the basins of the lakes were gouged out. Then as the ice receded for the last time, perhaps between 7,000 and 30,000 years ago, the basins filled and the Great Lakes were created. Now, an astounding 20% of all the freshwater in the world is contained within these five lakes!

In the present day, the westernmost point of New York State on Lake Ontario is Fort Niagara. Here, the Niagara River empties into the lake after churning over the world famous Niagara Falls. The Niagara River actually runs from Lake Erie to Lake Ontario, but oceanliner traffic moving between the two lakes must bypass the falls by going through the 27-mile-long Welland Shipping Canal. This runs through Canada from Port Weller on Lake Ontario to Port Colborne on Lake Erie.

The northeasternmost point of the lake is Cape Vincent, which sits like a sentinel between Lake Ontario and the beginning of the Thousand Islands section of the St. Lawrence River. Directly across from Cape Vincent is Kingston, Canada. Between the two lay several islands, the biggest being Wolfe Island, Canada. A ferry boat service exists between Cape Vincent, Wolfe Island, and Kingston, making it easy for anyone wishing to get quickly across to the Canadian mainland.

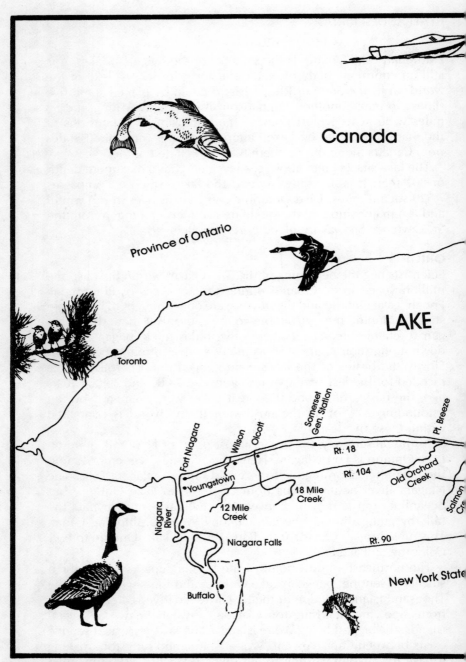

▶ 1a. LAKE ONTARIO

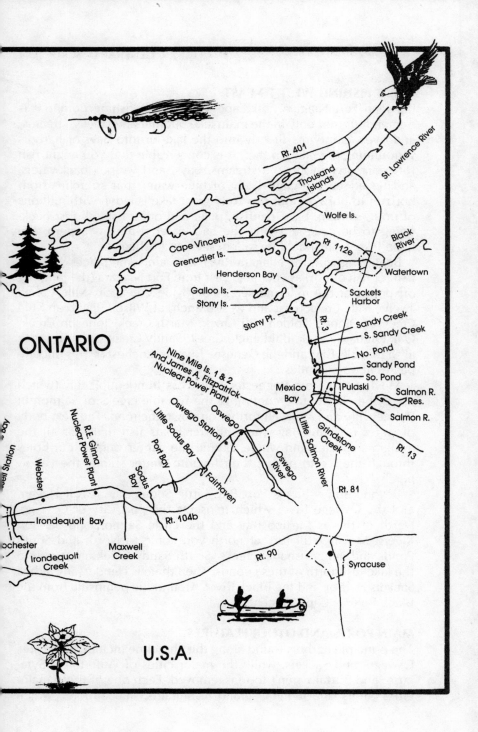

Rt. 401

Thousand
Islands

St. Lawrence River

Wolfe Is.

Rt 112e

Black
River

Cape Vincent

Grenadier Is.

Watertown

Henderson Bay

Sackets
Harbor

Galloo Is.

Stony Is.

ONTARIO

Stony Pt.

Rt. 3

Sandy Creek

S. Sandy Creek

No. Pond

Nine Mile Is. 1 & 2
And James A. Fitzpatrick
Nuclear Power Plant

Sandy Pond

So. Pond

Mexico
Bay

Pulaski

Salmon R.
Res.

Oswego

Salmon R.

Oswego Station

R.E. Ginna
Nuclear Power Plant

Little Sodus Bay

Grindstone
Creek

Rt. 13

Port Bay

Oswego
River

Little Salmon River

Webster

Sodus
Bay

Fairhaven

Rt. 81

Irondequoit Bay

Rt. 104b

ochester

Maxwell
Creek

Rt. 90

Irondequoit
Creek

Syracuse

U.S.A.

GREAT FISHING WEST TO EAST

Between Fort Niagara and Cape Vincent the fishing potential is tremendous, not only in the main lake but in many creeks, streams, and rivers emptying directly into the lake or into bays or harbors surrounding the lake. In fact, it is conceivable that you might fish for years, sticking to the streams, bays, and various backwaters, and never see the giant body of blue water that stretches from horizon to horizon. But this truly great lake is laden with millions of trout, salmon, bass, panfish, pike, and other fish, all just beckoning to be caught. While the backwater fishing is superb, the main lake itself should be sailed, seen and fished.

Beginning with the Niagara River, here are some places you can fish (or fish out of) as you head east from Fort Niagara (the jumping off point for the mile markers): Four Mile Creek, Six Mile Creek, Twelve Mile Creek (east and west branch) at Wilson, Eighteen Mile Creek at Olcott, Golden Hill Creek, Marsh Creek, Johnson Creek, Oak Orchard Creek, Bald Eagle Creek, Sandy Creek, Salmon Creek at Braddocks Bay, and the Genesee River in Rochester. This encompasses about 70 miles.

Moving east from Rochester, you cross Irondequoit Bay (which abuts the city) before coming to the fishable creeks of Salmon in Pultneyville and Maxwell further on down the road. The next body of water is Sodus Bay where charter boats fish daily for all the available species and where, during the winter, anglers cut holes through the ice to pursue their favorite winter staple, the yellow perch.

Beyond Sodus Bay is Port Bay, Little Sodus Bay at Fair Haven, and the Oswego River which transects the port City of Oswego. North of this is Mexico Bay and the Little Salmon and Salmon Rivers. Moving still further north you come to North and South Ponds and many fishable creeks. South Sandy Creek empties into the lake just north of these ponds. Then there is Henderson Harbor, Sackets Harbor, and the Black River. Around the peninsula from the Black River is Cape Vincent.

MAIN PORTS AND OTHER FEATURES

The principle harbors found along this shoreline include Rochester, Oswego, and Sackets, while the major cities of Watertown, Syracuse, and Buffalo aren't too far removed. Each one of these major cities offers fine lodging, grand restaurants, and airports, which

Lake Ontario's tributaries offer superb trout and salmon fishing at budget prices. Here, anglers try for salmon beneath the dam on the Oswego River.

make them easy to reach for the long distance traveler and fisherman alike. The port cities all offer fishing facilities, bait and tackle shops, guide services, and everything required to put together an enjoyable trip.

If this isn't enough, all along the shoreline are state parks, camping grounds, and boat launching facilities making it easy for the itinerant fisherman to pursue his favorite species. At many of these parks and at most inlets are broad, long, and efficient fishing piers allowing you to fish in either the lake on one side or the inlet on the other. Many of these structures jut well over ¼ mile into Lake Ontario.

From a safety standpoint, you're on good ground if you think of Lake Ontario as an ocean. Like any ocean, the big lake can get downright angry in an instant. Giant waves have on occasion proven to be too much for ocean going tankers, and these are big ships! For certain, only fast, seaworthy craft should venture offshore in search of cold water species like trout and salmon. On the other hand, cartoppers and row boaters up to 16 feet will have no problem

STEELHEAD

A strong, hard-fighting, highly sought strain of rainbow trout (technically a strain which is able to "imprint" a particular stream and later return to that stream from the lake at spawning time). Characterized by a slender, oblong body, the steelhead has a dark, dorsal coloration with silver-white sides and belly with many dark spots along its back and caudal fin. Steelhead average 8-13 pounds when entering streams to spawn from late November on into March. They strike both lures and bait all winter long.

CHINOOK SALMON ("King Salmon")

The largest of the salmon family, these pacific coast giants are presently nearing 50 pounds in Lake Ontario while averaging somewhere around 20 pounds. The largest chinook ever caught in the five great lakes came from Ontario. Best methods include deep trolling in summer (though the large ones are often hard to troll in mid-summer), and trolling near tributaries from August through October (the best time). Anglers wading streams during the annual spawning migration, mainly in September and October, do well on fish up to 40 pounds.

LAKE TROUT

Easily identified by its forked tail, lake trout are one of Ontario's more cooperative gamefish. Lakers are most often in 51-degree water, usually on the bottom near some kind of structure. Trolled most of the year on spoons, plugs and flies, there is also some shoreline fishing for lakers in spring. Fish from 8-10 pounds are quite common in early spring, while summer trollers take even bigger fish (up to about 20 lbs.). Primary baits used to catch this pale green char include alewife herring and smelt.

NORTHERN PIKE

This water wolf of the north country is found from the lower Niagara River all the way around to Cape Vincent. Possessed of a voracious appetite, a pike will eat just about anything and can be quite easily coaxed into striking. Six to eight pounders are common with fish in the 20's caught annually. Both live bait and lures are used. Prime time is early in the morning, especially in weedy, shallow backwaters. Speed trolling and deep jigging are other successful gambits. Ice fishing provides some additional sport on the battling northern.

SMALLMOUTH BASS

Lake Ontario was reknowned for its exceptional smallmouth fishing long before the big salmon came along. Fish in the three pound range are quite common, with fish over five pounds possible. Soft shelled crawfish ("crabs") make the best bait, while small plugs trolled six to eight feet behind bright cannonballs should quickly gain attention. Good to excellent catches are made all summer long, especially where the water remains quite cool (as in Henderson Harbor and the St. Lawrence River). Smallies are widely dispersed, but it pays to find some kind of rocky structure.

▶ **1b. PROFILES OF ONTARIO'S MAIN GAME FISH SPECIES**

COHO SALMON ("Silver Salmon")

The smaller of the two pacific salmon, coho delight anglers by striking a multitude of baits and lures trolled or fished still. Action occurs off piers and bulkheads early in the season then quickly moves offshore where these salmon (from 4-20 pounds) can be caught (although not in large number) all summer long. Coho spawn from September through October. In the early part of this period, anglers have good luck trolling for them near the mouths of rivers. Later on, they are caught in most tributaries.

MUSKELLUNGE

The largest member of the pike family, muskies are known for sharp teeth and great power. Perhaps the most famous musky region in the world is right here in Lake Ontario's Cape Vincent. Twenty pound fish are common, with much bigger fish possible. Musky fishermen casting lures and baits look for structure, water less than 15 feet deep, and gravel bottom. Many fish are caught while trolling large swimming plugs and spoons. Special fishing gear and a guide are recommended for the inexperienced. Muskies don't come easy.

BROWN TROUT

Stocked heavily all around the lake, browns reach 8-20 pounds in a remarkably short period of time. The mainstay of early spring "ice-out" fishermen, they're taken from shore or near shore on light tackle as soon as the ice disappears. These fish prefer 56-60 degrees of water where they are trolled all summer long. Brief runs are made from time to time into many of the tributaries, especially in the fall. Worms and minnows make excellent baits. Many of the largest browns are taken at night.

WALLEYED PIKE

Actually a large member of the perch family, this fish offers only fair opportunity in Lake Ontario and then only in select areas. Locally known as "yellow pike", "old marbleyes" or just "walleye", it makes fine tablefare. Many are caught incidentally by bass fishermen, but most are taken by trollers specifically fishing for them and using a nightcrawler or large minnow trailed behind a weight forward spinner. Jigs and minnows make excellent, summer deep-water baits. Best fishing hours are late afternoon and evening, best time is early spring and fall.

LARGEMOUTH BASS

Not as abundant as the smallmouth, largemouth are nonetheless fairly common in the backwaters of Lake Ontario. Although two to three pounders can be expected, bucketmouths up to five pounds are caught. These bass strike a wide variety of lures including surface plugs, stick baits, spinners, spinner-baits, buzzbaits, rubber worms, crankbaits and jigs. Early in the morning is good, as is dusk. But after dark is the best time to nail a 'hawg. Since the largemouth are relatively unmolested, in deference to the prized smallmouth, they tend to be quite cooperative.

whatsoever fishing in all the protected bays, creeks, and rivers surrounding the lake.

If you'd like to catch a few truly giant trophy fish, Ontario makes it easy — and cheap! Instead of being located in some remote end of the world, Lake Ontario is right here in New York State, only hours away from most east coast cities (see Fig. 5-a). The truth is, you no longer have to go to such places as New Zealand, Argentina, or even Alaska to catch that monster trout or salmon of a lifetime. And, whether you fly in, drive in, or come in by boat, all you might need to get in on the action will be right there at your finger tips.

Everything you need to know about this great fishing will be presented in the following chapters. And whether you're a good fisherman or not, we'll show you exactly where, when, and how Ontario can fulfill your wildest angling dreams.

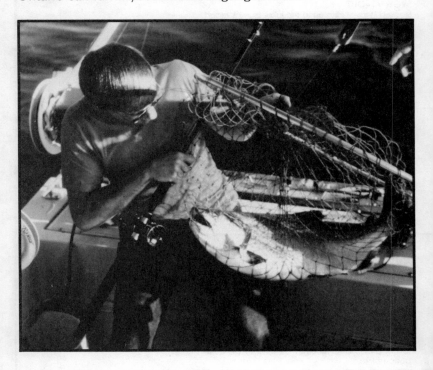

HISTORICAL PERSPECTIVE AND MANAGEMENT

*"The Chippewa still tell stories
of runs of fish up the rivers . . .
runs so thick that a man could
almost walk across them."*

▼
2

It is hard for some to imagine a body of water as far north as the Great Lakes being a major *year round* recreational fishing center. Yet, major important gamefish species are caught here during every month of the year! True, the winter can be downright disasterous with temperatures hovering in the sub-zero digits. However, ice fishing along with steelhead fishing in the Salmon River and other ice-free tributaries offer Lake Ontario anglers a winter potential realized by very few other northern areas. It hasn't always been this way.

EARLY INHABITANTS

Early records indicate that the region was first occupied by North American Indians. The Algonquin Tribes lived on the Canadian side of Lake Ontario and the St. Lawrence River, while the southern or New York side was inhabited by the Iroquois. Some of the more common Indian tribes in the north were the Montagnais, Cree, Ojibway (Chippewa), Malecite, and Naskapi. Of these tribes, the Montagnais and Naskapi were fishermen. They fished along many of the tributaries feeding either the St. Lawrence River or Lake Ontario. In the south, friends of the Iroquois were the more familiar Oneida, Onondaga, Cayuga, and Mohawks. Many regions, lakes, and rivers still bear the names of the olden tribes which once ruled this region.

Fishing and hunting was a way of life, a means of survival. Big game hunting was conducted in the fall and winter, and fishing was done for the most part during the spring and summer. Although records show attempts at hook and line angling, most Indian fishermen pursued their quarry with clubs and spears. Fishing to them meant food, not a means of escape from daily turmoil. Indian fishermen would hunt or search the river for fish. Once the fish were spotted, rough barriers, such as dams made out of logs, sticks, or reeds, would be positioned above and below them. Then, the fishermen would cast their spears and swing their clubs until all their food gathering was accomplished.

The Chippewa still tell stories of runs of fish up the rivers . . . runs so thick that a man could almost walk across them. Best accounts indicate that the major species of fish taken during these sorties to the tributaries included lake trout, eels, perch, walleyes, landlocked salmon, pickerel, smallmouth, and largemouth bass. Some of these fish lived in the tributaries year round, but some, like the lake trout and salmon were more lake oriented and only entered the rivers during certain periods to spawn or to feed on their favorite forage species. At times like these, the Indians would descend upon the rivers where they would trap and catch large numbers of the bigger fish.

With the discovery of the new world, European explorers soon set sight on Lake Ontario. Samuel de Champlain was known to have sailed along Ontario in the year 1615. During much of the 1600's, war raged in the region, as the French and English fought for control of this Iroquois country. Eventually, the English prevailed and trading posts sprung up along the lake as travel by water was then the easiest means. English rule ended, of course, after the Revolutionary War. But the region continued to grow and by the mid-1830's Buffalo, Rochester and Oswego had grown to sizable cities of 12,000 or more.

With little or no regard for the bountiful land which supported him so well, the new "landlord" of the territory, the white man, slowly and systematically degraded Lake Ontario and its tributaries. By the 1870's, the lake and surrounding territories had already undergone drastic change. Dams and deforested watersheds along with industrial and municipal pollution and over fishing caused great stress. Trout that had once been extremely plentiful were nearly eliminated. And in 1880, the salmon actually disappeared totally from the lake. It was a sad time!

LAKE ONTARIO HITS BOTTOM

By the mid-1930's, both the sport and commercial fisheries in the area were in a state of still further decline. Not only had they been overtaxed by poor environmental management, fishing, and poaching, but now a new calamity appeared on the scene. It took the form of the sea lamprey eel which entered Lake Ontario from the St. Lawrence River. This menace quickly spread from one great lake to another through the tremendous network of canals which had been dug in the preceding decades.

The sea lamprey eel is a parasitic fish which feeds on other "host" fish. It feeds by attaching itself to the side of its victim and slowly sucking out the fish's body juices. Eventually this will weaken, if not kill the host, whereupon the lamprey sets out to find a new victim. It attacks not only lake trout, but also rainbow and brown trout, walleye, bass, panfish...in fact, most freshwater fish. Growing up to a maximum of about three feet and a weight of three pounds (but averaging only 1 to 1½ lbs) these ravenous lampreys compounded the problems man had created in the Great Lakes.

By 1950, most of the lake trout had been decimated along with the native salmon. Then, in the face of lampreys and many other problems an association was formed: *The International Great Lakes Fishery Commission,* established in 1955. Their first endeavor was to figure out how to combat the sea lamprey.

Controls were established in Lakes Superior, Michigan, and Huron

Conservation officer examines a big chinook salmon at the mouth of the Little Salmon River.

by placing selective poisonous lampricides (which killed only juvenile lampreys) into the tributaries around where the beasts were known to spawn. Then, when the lampreys were finally in check, these lake regions set out on a new plan. With the help of the U.S. Fish and Wildlife service and with guidance from the Fishery Commission, the Great Lakes States began a lake trout restocking program.

In 1966, Michigan made the first successful attempt to stock Pacific coast salmon. These "king" (chinook) and "silver" (coho) salmon were planted in Lake Michigan. The overall desirability and apparent hardiness of these species prompted neighboring states to establish successful Pacific salmon programs in both Lakes Superior and Huron.

Spurred on by the other lakes' accomplishments, the Department of Environmental Conservation, the province of Ontario, and the U.S. Fish and Wildlife Service conducted experimental stockings in Lake Ontario and Lake Erie. However, the initial results indicated that there was still a rather gaudy lamprey problem. An extensive lamprey control program was initiated in Lake Ontario in 1971. Soon thereafter, the program showed it could control the parasite.

NEW HOPE FOR THE BIG LAKE

With the new control program well in place, Lake Ontario was again stocked with trout. Pacific coast salmon were next introduced and by the mid-70's, these experimental stockings had proven to be extremely successful. The big lake, in fact, demonstrated the poten-

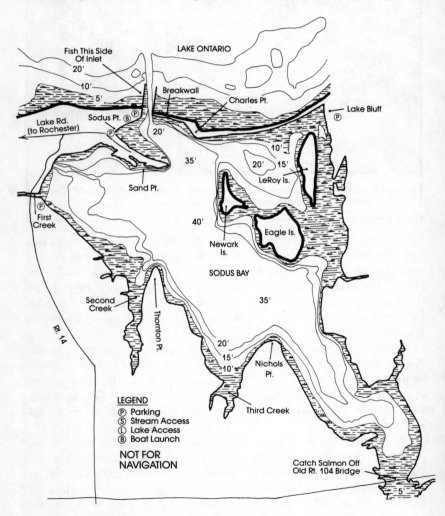

LEGEND
Ⓟ Parking
Ⓢ Stream Access
Ⓛ Lake Access
Ⓑ Boat Launch

NOT FOR
NAVIGATION

▶ 2a. SODUS BAY

tial to support some of the finest trout and salmon fishing in the world. But in order to maintain this newly developed and thriving program, two ongoing fisheries programs had to be established. One had to maintain leverage on the sea lamprey eel problem, and the second had to develop a hatchery system that could grow and stock young fish in Ontario.

The Fishery Commission committed its resources to control the Lake Ontario lamprey, and the DEC developed a statewide hatchery modernization program. This included the construction of the *Salmon River Fish Hatchery* (Altmar) and renovation and expansion of several other already existing hatcheries. With financial assistance offered by the federal government for the new hatchery through the Anadromous Fish Conservation Funds, Heritage Conservation and Recreation Funds, and the Dingell-Johnson Fish Restoration Funds, the construction of the new $11 million dollar Altmar facility was begun in 1977.

NEW SPECIES

Upon completion, the Salmon River Fish Hatchery began rearing for distribution into Lake Ontario and its tributaries chinook and coho salmon, steelhead and domestic rainbow trout, and brown trout. Today, in an ongoing effort to improve New York's fisheries program, Skamania strain steelhead are being reared and released into the big lake. This will introduce a new close-to-shore fishery for these great fighting fish, one that should last all summer long with an early spawning season slated to begin somewhere around September. At the same time, other fisheries attempts are being made to reintroduce landlocked salmon and to introduce "Bavarian Seeforellen", (a type of German Brown Trout which grows in excess of 50 pounds) to some New York State waters. If this experiment is successful, the giant browns will also be introduced into Lake Ontario.

In addition to all these efforts centered on the cold water fishery, other hatcheries have been placed on line to increase the numbers of warm water species available. Large and smallmouth bass, tiger muskies, muskellunge, and walleyes are all grown in hatcheries to help supplement the naturally occurring populations in the lake.

The story of Lake Ontario is certainly a great success story and a major triumph for modern fisheries management, but it isn't without qualification. True, all the major native species of fish have been reestablished, new species have been introduced, and they are all doing well. Yet the waters of Lake Ontario retain pollutants from a time when industry along the lake was less controlled. Some of the worst of these pollutants are PCB's, Mirex, and Dioxin, which exist in the water and are picked up by the plankton. These minute, free floating, life forms are fed upon by small forage species, which in turn are fed upon by still larger predatory game-fish. This natural food chain concentrates the pollutants in ever higher levels with the result that the most desirable, large gamefish, are most contaminated.

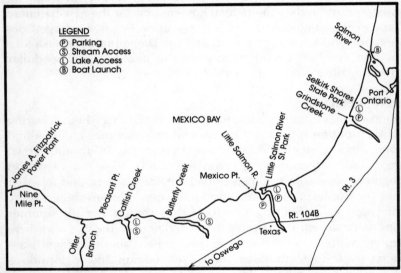

▶ *2b. MEXICO BAY*

IMPORTANT HEALTH ADVISORIES

Many anglers coming to Lake Ontario fish primarily for sport, and many release a share of the fish they catch. But if you plan to eat Lake Ontario fish, you should be aware of certain restrictions and advisories posted by the New York State DEC.

One such advisory is found on the back of the front cover of the New York State Fishing Regulations Guide. To minimize potential adverse health impact, the NYS Department of Health recommends that you "eat no more than one meal (½ pound) per week of fish from *any water in the state,*" with these further admonitions dealing specifically with Lake Ontario: For Lake Ontario, the St. Lawrence River, and the Niagara River below the falls do not eat any eels, channel catfish, lake trout, chinook salmon, coho salmon over 21 inches, rainbow trout over 25 inches, and brown trout over 18 inches and eat no more than one meal per month of white perch, smaller coho salmon, rainbow and brown trout.

It is further recommended that "women of childbearing age, infants, and children under the age of 15 should not eat fish with elevated contamination levels." It should be further stated that all the fish in Lake Ontario are deemed to have elevated contamination levels.

Just as the fishing in Lake Ontario was rejuvenated over a period of years, it will take time to restore the quality of water that existed in a yesteryear. Locations where pollutants have been entering the lake have been identified, and attempts are being made to clean them up. Mirex at one time was manufactured along the Niagara River and got into the lake. This process has been stopped. Another dangerous contaminant, dioxin, appeared in the manufacture of the defoliant 2,4,5,-T. It actually wasn't planned or necessary in the production and now with more careful manufacturing controls the problem is being eliminated. Finally, there has been a banning of the plasticizing polychlorinated biphenyls (PCB's), and now the natural processes of sedimentation (imbedding of the contaminates in silt), filtration (the removal of anything containing the pollutant) and bacteriological breakdown of the contaminants are lessening this menace.

In spite of the problems, no angler should miss the opportunity to get in on some of the finest fishing found anywhere in the world. Catch-and-release is now a common policy among enlightened sportsmen, and as far as eating the fish, the situation is improving all the time. Then, of course, there is that world record trout, salmon or musky that is swimming in Ontario and just dying to put your name in the book.

LAKE ONTARIO CALENDAR YEAR

"In winter, Ontario slumbers like an ice bear fringed with rime frost. But those months, like all the others, are alive with angling opportunity."

▼
3

In this chapter, we will give you a seasonal time reference for the various types of fishing found around the big lake and its tributaries without going into great detail. In later chapters, we will expound on every aspect of each important fishing season.

There is twelve-month-a-year fishing on Lake Ontario. Beginning each spring, the steelhead which have spent the winter holding over in tributaries around the lake and some fresh March runners spawn and exit the rivers. These fish attain remarkable size and strength, and fish in excess of 10 pounds are caught up until mid April. Often the fish taken are spawnouts, i.e. they may have been holding in a river for many months, but have only recently spawned. Those not caught return to the big lake and they do survive, unlike most Pacific salmon which die soon after spawning. Spawnouts tend to be big fish, but very thin. If they were still full of roe, they would weigh many more pounds upon being caught.

ICE OUT

As the early spring wears on, brown trout invade all inshore areas. These browns tend to follow the smelt from offshore into the river mouths,where they feed voraciously on these small, spawning fish. Anglers fishing along piers, inlets, or beaches do well during this time of year on browns that often weigh over eight pounds. Domestic rainbows, steelhead, cohos, and landlocked salmon usually move in along the southern tier and join the browns around late April.

The most common method used to catch brown trout along the shoreline is casting swimming plugs like the Countdown Rapala or spoons like the Little Cleo. Cast out as far as possible, and retrieve them back at a very slow rate of speed. If you intend to fish off a pier, remember that piers are usually rather high up and a long handled net will be necessary to lift your fish out of the water.

Fishing around warm water discharges is also highly productive during the early spring. A warm water discharge is a place where the steam and hot water produced by an electric power plant is reconverted back into water. At the discharge, the lake's water temperature is elevated several degrees and the gamefish come into the area to warm up and feed. However, the air temperature can remain extremely cold and the lake can be very rough even if the wind and weather cooperate. If you intend to come up in the spring, try to time your trip to hit the best weather or plan your trip to last several days so that if you get blown off the lake on a few of those days, you will still have some more on which to fall back. The inshore fishing usually holds up well for these species until late May.

Should the big lake prove to be too rough, trout and some salmon can be caught in the protected backwaters found around the southern shore and mentioned in Ch. 2. Any river, bay or harbor that can offer protection from the pounding waves can be counted on to give up a few trout during a day of fishing. Thus, even though the weather on the main lake is miserable, you still may be able to score with a good catch of trout.

Boat fishermen, however, must work extra hard in these bays if they intend to put together a good catch. This is especially true if they use side planer boards, which in essence make their craft up to 50 feet or more wide (see Ch. 6). When two boats approach each other and both are using these boards, many tricky maneuvers develop. Should a first time captain try to fish side planer boards in a small bay, small wars could erupt!

Another problem confronting captains in the bays is the vegetation and debris often found floating in the water. Good fishermen frequently stop and check their lures to make certain they haven't picked up any junk and are still operating properly. Side planer board fishing may be testing, but the rewards usually justify the effort.

In April, the weather can be counted on to take a turn for the better. The sun finally gets the opportunity to warm the water up some and the fish respond by becoming more active. Although more days are fishable than in March, still the majority are tough at best. This means that either the lake is rough, the air temperature is cold, the wind is blowing, or something else is affecting the fishing. But, if all the elements cooperate, limit catches of trout and salmon can be expected on some days.

While the lake conditions continue to improve, you can still count on the bays and backwaters for a few fish during this month. Limit catches in the bays aren't too common now, but since the bigger browns remain longer, you actually have an improved chance of catching an eight pound or better lunker. By contrast, boaters working the main lake during this particular season commonly make limit catches of trout (5 trout and salmon in aggregate per angler) with perhaps the biggest brown weighing in the 4-6 pound range. Now, that's not too shabby!

In May, the lake really begins to sizzle! Lake trout join the browns feeding in close. Often, these early season lakers will strike any lure pulled through the water and at this time limit catches of three fork-tails (lake trout) per angler are the rule. The lakers will average from 6-12 pounds and are fun to catch on light tackle. Also, along the shoreline big perch move in and are caught on worms and shiners.

TURN OVER

May weather usually cooperates. True, you can still have a bad day or two, but by this time of the year the good days begin to out-number the bad. As the water warms, the fish tend to move out of

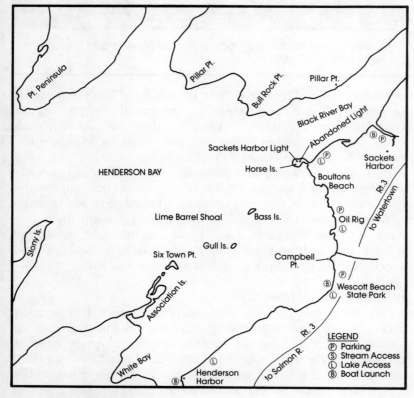

▶ **3a. HENDERSON BAY**

Spinning and baitcasting rods, polaroid glasses and the right lures add up to bass.

the backwaters and feed mainly in the big lake. Two other events that now usually occur and which tend to annually hurt fishing are (1) the lake turns over (see Ch. 7) and (2) a die-off of alewife herring occurs. The limit catches that were common during March, April, and early May are now much harder to make.

The walleye, pickerel, and northern pike season opens on the first Saturday in May. So, as the trout and salmon vacate the backwaters, these warm water species start to move in and become the dominant species. The walleyes are caught in many deep river channels, deep bays, and beyond inlets in the lake, while the pickerel and northerns are caught all along the shoreline and especially in all the adjoining ponds and river mouths.

OVERLOOKED FLY FISHING

During the month of June, some interesting trout fishing takes place in many streams emptying into Lake Ontario. However, instead of fish of monstrous proportions, 7-15 inch trout are what you will find. These are native and stocked fish that do not run all the way out to the lake. They can be seen rising freely to hatches of flies from the late spring on into summer, and good catches can be made by those anglers interested in pursuing these smaller fish. Dedicated fly fishermen can and should get in on this action.

While good trout fishing continues in the tributaries for these smaller fish, big brown trout, lake trout, and salmon begin to move offshore. Steelhead are caught way offshore up to five and six miles off the beach using planer boards and downriggers. Here, they congregate around thermal bars (also called thermal barriers). In closer to the beach, side planer boards are stowed away, and the fishery takes on a different trolling posture with downriggers fully in force. Good catches of brown and lake trout are common.

Late in June, the bass and muskellunge seasons open and many fishermen come to Lake Ontario specifically in pursuit of these excellent fighting fish. Many muskies over 25 pounds are caught annually, smallmouth bass average well over 1½ pounds with many fish exceeding four pounds, while the largemouth bass fishing is good with many fish caught in excess of four pounds.

During the summer, most species of Ontario fish can be caught with regularity somewhere in the lake. Inshore, panfish are absolutely everywhere! Smallmouth bass can be caught along most beaches, cold water fishing for lake trout really takes off, and brown trout can be found in their preferred temperature zone. The one exception is the large chinook salmon, which seem to go into hibernation and virtually disappear from fish catches around the lake (to find them, see Ch. 13); smaller chinook, land-locks (from experimental stockings) and cohos are caught with surprising regularity.

TIME OF THE GIANT

As the days of summer begin to shorten during the month of August, more and more salmon begin showing up along the coast. They especially gravitate to the front of the major tributaries, into which they will start their annual spawning run sometime during the month of September. Trollers change over from fishing for lakers and begin in earnest trying to catch a few chinook to 40 pounds and many cohos to 20 pounds. Although the coho salmon population seems to fluctuate from year to year, it is common in a good season to put more than a dozen of these fine fighting and eating fish on ice during a single day trip.

Other species such as brown and lake trout can also be caught mixed with the salmon. Later, the browns will enter the rivers with the salmon and feed heavily upon eggs which will be set free during the spawning process.

Degrees F.	
80	WARM WATER SPECIES
79	
78	Bullheads, Channel Catfish
77	
76	White Bass
75	Bluegills
74	
73	
72	Largemouth Bass
71	Crappies
70	Northern Pike
69	
68	Smallmouth Bass, Yellow Perch
67	Walleyes, Muskies
66	
65	
64	
63	COLD WATER SPECIES
62	
61	
60	Brown Trout
59	
58	Rainbow Trout
57	
56	
55	
54	Chinook & Coho Salmon
53	
52	
51	Lake Trout
50	

▼
3b.
*OPTIMAL TEMPERATURES
FOR LAKE ONTARIO SPECIES*

All during this late-summer, early-fall period, smallmouth bass fishing is excellent. The best approach is to use live crayfish ("crabs") for bait and to fish for the bass in from 15-30 feet of water over rocky bottom areas. Inlets like the mouth of the Salmon River will be crawling every evening with smallmouth waiting for crustaceans and small herring to get washed out into the big lake as the hydro-electric generating plant heavily increases the flow of the river.

WORLD CLASS MUSKY FISHING

Further to the north near Cape Vincent, muskellunge activity begins to increase as September arrives. Time of day is not of paramount importance to muskellunge fishermen, but perhaps the best action comes somewhere around mid-day. There are three other important factors involving the muskellunge fishery, and they are the same as in real estate: location, location, and location. If you can find 10-15 feet of water with a heavy gravel and rock bottom, you may find a trophy fish lurking somewhere in the neighborhood. Cape Vincent does, indeed, exhibit this type of bottom structure, and the musky fishing is considered among the best in the region .

As September begins to roll in, you can look for the salmon to start their annual spawning run up any tributary that is sporting enough water to hold the fish. Often, only a few rivers and streams entering the lake have enough water in them during this time of year to support a good September run. However, all it takes is a good rain or two to swell the tributaries and get the famed run started. But, no matter what the rain conditions, the Salmon River, the Black River, the Genesee River, and the Niagara River will all see runs of salmon beginning sometime during this month.

Also during September, northern pike, walleyes, bass and muskellunge begin feeding heavily in anticipation of the impending winter. Look for increased action to follow the first frost and should the weather turn cold early, the action may last right on up until ice-in conditions. Since it gets cool sooner further north, the St. Lawrence River fishing picks up well during the latter part of the month with northern pike, muskellunge, and smallmouth bass providing the bulk of the activity.

Throughout September and well on into October, the salmon mount increasingly strong surges into the rivers. Salmon fishermen score well on fresh run chinook and coho salmon. But then, like everything else, this river fishing ends. The lake gets very cold and rough and it becomes increasingly difficult to find and catch any salmon. However, one river that does hold up better than all the rest during this late season is the Genesee River in Rochester.

In the Genesee, fresh salmon just in from the lake continue to be caught right on through October by trollers. Trollers work from just outside the mouth of the river on up to the city proper of Rochester and make good catches of fresh chinook salmon *averaging* some-

▶ *Don't pass up some of the smaller creeks. Many offer fine steelheading, and crowds will be less. An elbow pool is a good place to look for the winter king.*

where around 20 pounds a fish. Once this action abates, the winter cycle is about ready to begin. Fresh snow again starts to fall in the area, the lake becomes extremely rough, and for all intents and purposes, the only sane fishing that can be done is in the tributaries.

As the inshore river mouths and bays start freezing up, ice fishermen begin getting their gear ready for the November 15th opening of their season. Any water sporting enough ice to support the weight of a contingent of anglers is a good bet to get heavy fishing pressure for the rest of the winter season. The major species sought is the omnipresent yellow perch. However, northern pike, trout, and pickerel can make things interesting. Since it gets extremely cold everywhere in this northern wonderland, winter dress is very important.

STAMINA AND STEELHEAD
In winter, Ontario slumbers like an ice bear fringed with rime frost. But these months, like all the others, are alive with angling opportunity.

Inland, beginning sometime in October, the "lakerun" rainbow trout or "steelhead" begin invading all the running tributaries. Fish up to 24 pounds are caught as they make their way upstream to where they intend to wait for the right conditions to spawn anytime from December on through mid April. The run usually peaks near Christmas.

When these beautiful, sleek fish first enter the tributaries, they are bright silver in color. However, the longer they remain in the rivers, the darker they get. Eventually they become almost black, with a dull red streak running along their mid-section from their operculum down to their pectoral fin. They are very aggressive fish and will strike passing clusters of salmon eggs, spawn bags, flies, miniature marshmallows and lures. Their democratic tastes and hard fighting qualities make them excellent targets for the winter fisherman.

Sometimes the hardest part of steelheading can be just getting to the river. Winter can cover the ground with up to five feet of snow or more, and since the majority of secondary tributaries all freeze over, only the Niagara, Genesee, Oswego, and Salmon River offer fishing for steelhead for the most part of the winter. However, eventually snow and ice conditions will prevent anglers from even getting into the Niagara and Genesee Rivers, and then most steelhead activity will switch over to the famed Salmon River in and around the Village of Pulaski.

The Salmon River never freezes over from the rapids above the Port Ontario Route #3 bridge upstream as long as it receives its daily rush of fresh water from the deep Salmon River Reservoir. The water, which is used to generate electricity and has a temperature somewhat above 32 degrees Fahrenheit, washes away any snow and ice that may have accumulated along the river's banks overnight. The warmer water also makes it a little easier for the steelhead fisherman, who must often wade in waist-deep water, trek through woods clogged with snow and ice and contend with an air temperature that's usually hovering in the low to mid-teens.

This becomes a fisherman's fishery! For one thing, if you don't know what you are doing, there's little chance that you would even attempt to fish during this often bitter time of the year. However, for those very interested in catching a few steelhead while not crazy enough to wade into the wintry river, there are guide boat services which drift the river daily in MacKenzie River Drift Boats.

Drift boats usually start sailing for steelhead around the first week of November. This is an interesting way to see large sections of the river, while avoiding the risk to life or limb while wading in treacherous, icy currents. These trips must have high water in order to operate. Should the power plant not be allowing any water to come through the dam, the boats would not be able to sail. But, as is often the practice during the late winter, the plant runs water twenty-four hours a day continuously and the drift boats get a good opportunity to run down the river.

This Salmon River steelhead fishing usually holds up into the early spring. Boat anglers and waders alike take at least some fish until the steelhead leave the rivers sometime around the middle of April. As for the many smaller creeks between Fort Niagara and Cape Vincent, wading fishermen try to be the first into them after the ice breaks. These intrepid souls have a good opportunity to catch fresh steelhead and many others that have wintered over in these creeks and rivers.

That takes us around the remarkable calendar year on Lake Ontario and its tributaries. Starting with Ch. 6, you can turn to the area that interests you most. However, the next two chapters will provide a great deal more useful information intended to make your Lake Ontario expedition a complete success.

NO EXPERIENCE NECESSARY

"With absolutely no experience, an angler might take a 30-pound chinook, a 15-pound coho, a 12-pound laker and a 10-pound brown... all on the same day."

4

Whether you are a seasoned pro or just a beginner, you'll find that Lake Ontario has something to offer everyone. Even if you don't own a shred of fishing tackle, you can participate — and do well! There is a myriad of charter boat services all around the lake. Once you arrange a charter, the captain and crew will do as much as they have to do in order to assure a successful and enjoyable day. The more experienced you are, the progressively less they will do; should you be a true beginner, they will do virtually everything except reel the fish in for you.

MAIN PORTS OF CALL

Beginning at the Niagara River, and heading east, charter boats operate out of: Youngstown on the Niagara River; Wilson; Olcott; Rochester; Sodus Point; Port Bay; Little Sodus Bay in Fair Haven; Oswego; the Little Salmon River; North and South Pond; Henderson Harbor; Sackets Harbor; and Cape Vincent (see Fig. 1-a). Not only do captains sail out of all these ports, but most, on occasion, trailer their boats to where the action is. Don't be surprised then if you call your captain a week before your scheduled charter and he says he will meet you at some other neighboring port.

It's relatively easy to make a charter boat connection. Since it is impossible to list all the captains currently operating, you would be best advised to contact the Chamber of Commerce and Visitor Bureau in the area in which you are most interested. Just ask for the phone numbers of any charter boat captains registered with them. They might even have a recommendation for a particular captain or service, so don't be afraid to ask. An alternative is to request of the C.O.C. the name or number of a local tackle shop operating in the area in which you want to fish. Most shops maintain lists of reputable captains with whom they do business.

When booking a charter, make certain to get in touch with a captain well ahead of time. These guys, especially the better ones, book up fast, so choice dates on a Saturday or Sunday are almost impossible to get. In some cases, you may be wise to book close to a year in advance. This isn't out of the ordinary. Of course, if you can sail on a weekday, this will make things easier and your lead time can be cut back considerably.

Before calling a captain, you should be aware of what types of charters are available and their approximate costs. All prices go up, of course, but the following figures will help you make some comparisons. Trip options available to you are: 4 hours or half day from $150 to $200; 6 hours or half day from $185 to $340 (these half-day trips can be arranged to depart either AM or PM hours); 7 hours from $250 to $400; and 8 hours $270 to $420. These prices usually reflect a 4-man charter. Captains will request from $40 to $50 dollars more per extra man up to a 6-man charter. Many captains cater to fishermen and their families, so do consider bringing your spouse and kids. Finally, make certain when discussing a trip with a captain whether you are discussing a 4 or 6 hour half day, or a 7 or 8 hour all day charter!

By the way, these considerable price differences exist because the size and accommodations of your charter boat will vary. Some of the skippers work small 18 foot center consoles. Others run extra large 32-footers (some with air-conditioning and stereo). The larger the boat and more luxurious the accommodations the greater the cost! For entertaining business people, or for special occasions, the captain will provide just about anything you're willing to pay for.

Another thing that might be mentioned while you are discussing a charter with a captain is "eight hours or limit." This means that if you and your three friends or family have contracted for an 8-hour trip and you catch your limit of trout and salmon in a shorter period of time, your contract has been successfully fulfilled and you may be on your way back to the dock. Of course, you can release some fish as you catch them, thereby prolonging your trip. But the best thing is just to be honest with the captain. Tell him what you want, and make sure you both understand what the arrangement is before you sail. Always know your options and don't be afraid to ask questions. Ask why so much or so little, and make certain you understand how many people you can bring along for the price and how much each additional angler will cost.

More times than not, your charter captain will work hard for you and will keep you out longer than what you've contracted for. This is especially true if things haven't been going too well. But, for everyone's sake, it is best to know exactly what to expect for the money you're about to commit.

After contracting a captain, he will require a small deposit to hold your date. Again, you should ask how much time you must give him to cancel your date and still get your deposit back. Also ask about weather considerations. What happens if there's a storm and you don't think it would be too safe to go out? Who has the

Lake trout charters are usually very successful, so bring along the family or friends.

final say, and what happens to the deposit? All captains have different policies, too numerous to mention. Make certain to ask questions so you can control the situation and forestall any later surprises.

LICENSE REQUIREMENTS
When going out on a charter from the U.S. side, you will need a new York State Fishing License. Currently, a resident license costs $9.50 for the year (which runs 10/1 to 9/30 of the following year). A non-resident license costs $27.50 or $15.50 for a special 5-day permit. Other things you will require are soft sole shoes, motion sickness medication if you are prone to sea sickness, sunglasses, a hat, raingear or coat, camera, lunch and drink, money for a tip (should you be later satisfied with the mate's and captain's performance) and a cooler for your fish once you get off the boat. We have spoken to several airlines and they have informed us that a cooler full of fish can travel in baggage if properly packaged and secured (see Ch. 20).

RIVER GUIDES

As for river charters, the most common one is the winter steelhead driftboat trip. However, if you want to wade the river you can hire a good river fishing guide who will take you on foot to the better pools and show you what to do. To contact either a drift boat captain or river fishing guide just call any tackle shop in the area you want to fish. They will be glad to furnish the names and numbers of local captains and guides who specialize in these types of fishing.

On a typical driftboat trip, you will pay $200 for two. That's $100 per man, admittedly not a cheap day on the water. But the trip runs between 6-8 hours with all the tackle supplied. A riverside lunch is provided, and the captain works his tail off actually rowing all day against the current. Since you can't move around too much in the driftboat, you better dress warm! Pocket warmers, thermal seats, and good thermal winter clothing are all necessities.

River fishing guides get up to $100 a day guaranteed for 1-2 anglers and up to $50 more for each additional angler. Their services may be acquired from September through April during the salmon and steelhead season, and their fees usually include transportation (from your motel to the fishing spots), tackle if required, and cleaning the catch. They will take you to the good spots, but it will be up to you to catch the fish. Often, this is easier said than done, so the guide fishes right along with you and attempts to add to your total catch.

WHAT TO EXPECT

If you've never been on a Great Lakes boat charter, it's natural to wonder what will take place. We'll discuss a typical one here, but remember that in Chapters 6-15 we'll also discuss many aspects of charter boat fishing.

Let's say it's your very first time. It won't hurt at all to make the captain aware of this, because then from the start he will probably go out of his way to explain everything he is doing. He will indicate which lures are better, water temperatures at different depths, and so on. Once the lines are out and a fish strikes, either the captain or the mate may grab the rod and hook the fish (or instruct you to do the same). Then, they will turn the rod over to you or a member of your party to fight the fish. If it's a big chinook, the fight just might last an hour or more! But, in most cases, after a reasonable struggle,

Type of Bait	Species Used On	Period Usually Available From Local Baitshops	How Sold	Methods to Catch (or make) Yourself
Nightcrawlers	All panfish, bass and trout	Live, spring to fall	Often 12/ carton live; preserved	Wet lawns, with flashlight at night
Crabs (soft crayfish)	Perch, bass, trout and freshwater drum	Live, spring to fall	Live by the dozen; preserved	Old meat wrapped in burlap or cheesecloth (claws grab and they get tangled)
Suckers, Chubs	Muskellunge, pike	Not available	—	Hook and line with worm for bait in rivers and creeks
Minnows (many species, including buckeyes, silver shiners, and others)	All species	Year round	By the dozen or preserved	Minnow trap in ponds, streams
Alewife Herring (Sawbelly)	Trout, bass and salmon	April to October (when available)	By the dozen	Umbrella nets or seine, usually at night with light
Egg Sacs	Trout and salmon	Year round	12 in vial	Wrap Salmon eggs in nylon mesh
Grubs (mousies, white grubs, spikes, mealworms, etc.)	All panfish, some trout (popular for ice fishing)	Year round (when available)	Package of 30 or preserved	Larval worms found in decaying logs, vegetation, top soil
Frogs	Bass, some panfish	Not available	Occasionally sold preserved	Along ponds or lakes with seines or by hand (or tempt with a dangling lure off rod)
Shrimp	Panfish	Not usually available in Ontario area	Preserved	Not available
Salamanders	Bass, pike, muskellunge	Not available	Preserved	Found along edges of rivers and ponds under objects
Hellgrammites	Bass and trout	June to October (when available)	Per piece	Live in rocky streams — Catch on wire mesh screen after dislodging rocks upstream
Caddis Worms	Trout	Not available	—	Gather by hand in streams — Many caddis resemble little twigs, found on bottom
Miscellaneous Insects — Crickets, Grasshoppers, etc.	Panfish, some trout	Not available	Preserved	Catch by various means
Ribbon Leeches	Bass, pike and muskellunge	June to October (when available)	By the dozen	Coffee can or burlap sack — Bait with fish heads, beef kidney or liver

· Always be sure to check regulations concerning the taking of bait!
· Preserved baits usually available year-round where sold.
· Not all tackle shops carry a wide variety of baits.

▶ **4a. NATURAL BAIT USED IN LAKE ONTARIO AND TRIBUTARIES**

the fish will succumb to your rod pressure and you'll have him near the boat.

At this point, the captain will reach for the net and you will be asked to lead the fish into it. After landing the fish, the captain will unhook and stow it away on ice. If you are going to take pictures, now is the time. A live fish looks infinitely better in a photo than a dead one.

If you are a knowledgeable fisherman, and if you are aware of how to react to a tripped downrigger rod, most captains will allow you to grab the rod and strike the fish. From that point on, you will battle the fish while the captain or mate will tend the net. The reason why most captains prefer netting all the fish, rather than allowing their fares to do it, is that should the lure pull out of the fish at the last moment, only they will risk being hooked. This is a very wise policy, because many anglers beginning or experienced just aren't aware of the danger in the force generated by pulling a lure out of a large struggling fish. Lures have been known to get deeply embedded in either face or hand! If you're an experienced angler out on a charter, most captains will allow you to unhook your catch and place it on ice.

Of course, the final chore performed by the captain and mate is to clean your fish. If you have any trophy fish for the wall, make certain to point out which ones you want to be mounted before the cleaning process begins. These fish will have to be separated and handled differently than the fish you intend to eat.

Anglers try for steelhead early in the morning from the pier and jetty in Selkirk Shores State Park.

If you have ever yearned to catch huge trout or salmon, but thought you'd have to travel to Alaska or other exotic places far beyond your means, a Lake Ontario charter just might be for you. With absolutely no experience you could conceivably take a 30 pound or better chinook salmon, a 15 pound coho salmon, a 12 pound lake trout, and a 10 pound brown all on the same day. As you're probably aware, some people fish for the better part of a lifetime and never catch one freshwater fish of such proportions. A big bonus is that if you have the time and would like to do some traveling, you and your family can take in the reknowned Niagara Falls or the Thousand Islands section of the St. Lawrence River — as well as much other beautiful scenery — on any trip to Lake Ontario.

Although many captains can and will set up motel or hotel reservations, a travel agent can secure everything including transportation for you. You can thus arrange for a charter or river fishing guide on a particular date and allow your agent to do the rest. Or you can allow the captain to make all the arrangements at the lake, while you handle all the travel details either by yourself or with the aid of an agent.

We hope this chapter has shown you that anyone of almost any age, even those with no fishing experience, can score big at Lake Ontario. But if you do care to go on your own, on the lake or especially on the streams, the next chapter will provide much useful data. Also in the next pages, we'll tell you about the exceptional range of restaurants, accommodations, and other services found in this sportsman's mecca.

MORE TRIP-PLANNING AIDS

"One Texas oil magnate comes up every year for the giant salmon. He can afford to go to Alaska — if not <u>buy</u> Alaska — but he knows he doesn't have to any more."

There's no place in the world that offers such fabulous fishing and is so close to so many people! Since Lake Ontario is less than 1500 miles away from the tip of Florida, it is relatively easy to reach from anywhere along the eastern seaboard of the United States. If you intend to drive up, Fig. 5-a shows mileages from most east coast cities. Maps in this and other chapters will further help you get to where you're going in the Lake Ontario region.

Ontario is so hot right now that people are flying in. One Texas oil magnate comes up every year for the giant salmon. He can afford to go to Alaska — if not buy Alaska — but he knows he doesn't have to any more. There are major airports at Buffalo, Rochester, Syracuse, Watertown and Oswego (major fly-in routes are shown on Fig. 5-b). All these cities are very convenient to the lake, and at the airports, car rental agencies are available. Optionally, most captains will agree to pick you up at the airport and get you to a motel where they will meet you on the morning of your charter.

WHERE TO STAY

As with charters, room reservations should be made well in advance. Most captains will supply nearby motel and hotel information and, if asked, may even make arrangements for you. The length of your trip may well depend upon how far you will have to travel. Obviously, if you are flying in from Texas or some other distant point, you'll try to stay longer. You may book charters for more than one day, and you may have a few days in between. What, then, will you do without a car? The bottom line is that if you fly in you're best off renting a car even if your captain offers to do some chauffeuring.

Accommodations are available all around the lake. Motels, hotels, guest houses, and lodges found lakeside cater to fishermen and are very convenient. They are usually near the major ports or right on the most widely fished streams. Many of these facilities offer coffee and doughnuts for breakfast but if you want more there are diners nearby. Some of the diners are open 24 hours a day and serve breakfast, lunch, and dinner. At most boarding houses and fishing lodges you can arrange for three meals a day. Scattered throughout the area there are also fine restaurants offering good menus for lunch and dinner.

It is always best to check for breakfast locations on the night

To Watertown	To Buffalo	From
466	548	Portland (ME)
389	471	Boston (MA)
371	453	Concord (NH)
157	423	Montpelier (VT)
220	302	Albany (NY)
290	377	Hartford (CT)
376	458	New York (NY)
350	450	Newark (NJ)
332	392	Philadelphia (PA)
449	219	Pittsburgh (PA)
428	368	Baltimore (MD)
471	511	Richmond (VA)
676	476	Charleston (WV)
853	653	Lexington (KY)
635	331	Columbus (OH)
500	270	Detroit (MI)
661	431	Fort Wayne (IN)
775	555	Chicago (IL)
991	761	Knoxville (TN)
968	738	Charlotte (NC)
1000	945	Charleston (SC)
1242	1126	Jacksonville (FL)
1215	985	Atlanta (GA)
1247	872	Birmingham (AL)
1593	1478	Miami (FL)
1491	1116	Jackson (MS)

▶ *5a. APPROXIMATE ROAD MILEAGE TO LAKE ONTARIO GATEWAY — Many visiting fishermen stay in Syracuse, Rochester or Oswego. These three cities fall between Watertown and Buffalo and so may be up to several hundred miles closer or farther depending on your origination point.*

before your trip. Often these restaurants get very crowded in the morning. We have waited, on occasion, for close to an hour just to be seated (add another half hour to get waited on and still more time before your food is prepared). Thus, it is best to check diner locations, opening times, and crowd situations ahead of time, and to get to the diner good and early. You want your big day to start off right.

There are things to watch out for when acquiring a room. For one, many local residents have partitioned their homes into extra rooms. Often, beds aren't the greatest, ventilation is poor, and most only offer a common rest room. Not quite the place to bring your family! Some hotels have similar problems. However, there are plenty of modern hotels and motels where all conveniences are available. The problem is that these better places will get booked early. One year, I wanted to book into a popular motel on the Salmon River for the first week of October . . . the time of the famed salmon run. I called in June to arrange for the room and fortunately received the last room in a 50 unit motel for the dates I required.

▶ *State launch ramps may be found all around the lake. This one is at Sodus Point.*

The point is to call early and be sure to ask questions about available facilities. Fishing is obviously a big business and Chambers of Commerce and Visitor Bureaus have large lists of reputable hotels and motels found in their areas.

Besides hotels, motels, guest houses, and lodges, there are State Parks and private campgrounds found all along the shoreline. Many of these facilities offer ramps where cartop or trailered boats can be launched into the lake. Also, nearby inlets often accommodate fishermen with convenient tackle shops and boat liveries renting boats and motors. Therefore, whether you trailer your own boat or not, you can still plan to get out and do a little fishing on your own.

Boat launch ramps for a fee can be found wherever there's a marina. Since this is a true waterland, marinas are all over. Yet state parks and public launching ramps are also available and at these facilities, you can usually launch for free. Some state parks have an entrance fee to park, but the nominal cost is well worth it. Rest rooms, adequate parking, and fish cleaning facilities will be available. During the summer, get to these places early, because parking will be at a premium. Remember, if you intend to go out onto the big lake, you should have a seaworthy boat. If you don't have such a craft, you should plan to fish right along the shore.

MAKING THE MOST OF YOUR STAY

Whether you are flying or driving in, if you have some extra days plan to fish on your own the day before your charter. Then stay over and fish the charter the next day. If you can come up for three days, bracket the charter in the middle. If you can't, then plan to leave for home immediately after the charter.

For your extra day, you will have to bring along your own tackle, especially if you intend to fish in the surf, at an inlet or in a stream or river. For bait and specific information, there are tackle shops spread out (in some places, side by side) all around the lake. These shops are generally well equipped with everything you will need. Rods and reels are available, as are waders, cleats, polaroid glasses, insect repellent, lures and other gear. Many of the ambitious shop owners in the area are also charter boat captains or river fishing guides. When you ask for information, they can really supply it. Don't be afraid to ask for a map, so they can further pin-point good locations. If you want, you can ask for lure recommendations or anything else you may require at that time. You can also call area hotlines for further fishing information (see Fig. 5-c.)

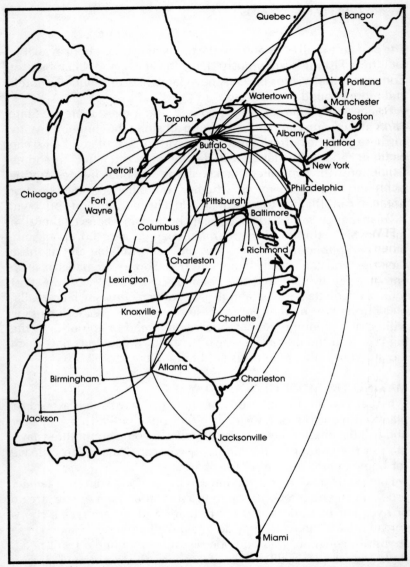

▶ *5b. MAIN FLYWAYS INTO LAKE ONTARIO — This map depicts airline routes into the Lake Ontario region. Usually, these routes will be without a plane change but there may be stops along the way. Buffalo and Watertown were selected because they are at opposite ends of the lake. Most cities connect into Buffalo, but for Watertown, you may want to connect through other major cities as shown. Syracuse and Rochester are also important gateways.*

OTHER HELPFUL LITERATURE

Besides tackle shops, you can also get great seasonal information concerning the big lake in such popular magazines as *Great Lakes Fisherman*, *New York Sportsman*, *Fly Fisherman*, *New York Game & Fish*, *Fly Fishing*, *The In-Fisherman*, *New York Fish Finder*, *The Salmon-Trout-Steelheader*, and *The Fisherman* (Long Island, New England, and New Jersey editions). Many of these publications offer sections devoted totally to Lake Ontario. All offer frequent feature articles dealing with one or more specific Ontario locations or techniques. Now, even the big national magazines like *Field & Stream* and *Sports Afield* are running Ontario features.

A FEW CHECKLISTS

When you fish on a charter, everything is supplied for you. But if you come on your own, you must be prepared. Towards that end, here are a few checklists that should help, starting with river fishing.

Checklist for river fishing on your own:

1. Waders or hip boots
2. Insect repellent (summer only)
3. Polaroid sun glasses
4. Wading staff
5. Cleats, like Walt's Walkers, for your boots
6. Fishing vest
7. Rain gear
8. Extra warm and dry clothing
9. Ice chest
10. Legal lures (check river regulations for number of hooks allowed on lures)
11. Tackle box with hooks (check river regulations for hook gap size), swivels, and sinkers
12. New York State Fishing Regulations Guide

Checklist for shoreline lake fishing on your own:

1. Folding chair
2. Long handled net
3. Insect repellent
4. Wind breaker
5. Thermal clothing if cold

The angler planning to visit Lake Ontario is fortunate to have a list of area fishing hotlines that he can call to get up to the minute reports on local fishing conditions. These reports cover both lake and tributary conditions, and include weather data, which species are being caught and best location.

Monroe County . . . . (716) 467-7320
Wayne County . . . . (315) 483-4454
Orleans County . . . . (716) 682-4223
Oswego County . . . . (315) 342-5873
Niagara County . . . . (716) 433-5606
Jefferson County . . . . (315) 782-2663

▶ *5c LAKE ONTARIO ANGLER HOTLINES*

6. Waders for surfcasting
7. Ice chest
8. Rain gear
9. Rod and reel combination that will enable long accurate casts
10. Tackle box with lures, hooks, swivels, and sinkers

As we discussed earlier, if you have a free day, do plan to fish. However, there are alternatives. Let's say you don't want to cart up everything required to fish on your own. You may just want to sightsee. By arriving a day early, you have a choice. The best part about fishing or just plain sightseeing the day before your charter is that you always meet many interesting people along the way. These people and their stories can get you very excited about your charter and perhaps even answer a few questions concerning your chances of catching fish. Of course if you do fish, you may catch a trophy before even stepping foot on your hired boat!

Finally, you may want to trailer your own boat to the lake or you may already have one docked there. In this case, you should be aware of the additional gear that you may require in order to have a successful trip:

Checklist for boating on your own:

1. Navigational charts
2. Compass or loran unit

3. Polaroid sun glasses
4. Life preservers
5. Rain gear
6. Extra dry and warm clothing
7. Food and drink
8. Ice chest
9. Wide assortment of lures
10. Extra line
11. Wide assortment of terminal tackle such as swivels, weights, and snaps
12. Sturdy rods capable of handling up to 20 pound test line
13. Extra reel or two
14. Large landing net
15. Good anchor and over 250 feet of anchor rope
16. Fire extinguisher
17. Good set of tools
18. Perhaps an extra spark plug or more
19. Downriggers (explained in Ch. 11)
20. Good fish finder (explained in Ch. 11)
21. Good camera
22. VHF or CB radio

FABULOUS FISHING ON THE SMALLEST GREAT LAKE

PART II

ICE-OUT FISHING

"When the ice moves out, the baitfish move in and the big browns follow to ravage the shoreline. The biggest brown ever taken in New York fell here."

6

Soon after the ice disappears from the surface of the shoreline and coves around Lake Ontario, some of the most interesting fishing of the entire year begins. This is primarily for lunker brown trout, but oftentimes coho salmon, lake trout, landlocked salmon and rainbow trout get mixed in, too. No one is ever quite sure when ice-out will happen, but for the most part, it occurs sometime during the month of March.

When the ice moves out, the baitfish move in and the big browns follow to ravage the shoreline. The biggest brown ever taken in New York fell here.

Comprised mostly of smelt, the baitfish make their way into the shallow shoreline waters and rivers immediately after ice-out to spawn. The larger gamefish follow directly behind them in hot pursuit of an easy meal.

THE BIG BROWNS ARRIVE

Not native to the Americas, the "German Brown" trout was introduced here in 1883. Usually averaging less than two pounds in streams, the brown trout can grow to lunker proportions in large bodies of water. The world rod and reel record now stands at over 35 pounds.

Soon after being stocked in Lake Ontario, browns lose their characteristic brown color and change to all silver sides with dark, spotlike markings. This is very similar to the landlocked salmon, but confusion should not occur because a landlocked salmon has many "X" markings on its side. Further, the brown trout has a double row of well developed vomerine teeth in the roof of its mouth, while the landlocked salmon has what appears to be one row that is not usually too well developed.

The browns are fairly active in water ranging from 52-66 degrees, but they have a preference for 56-60 degrees of water if they can find it. Ontario provides these ideal temperatures, and the fish feed voraciously reaching weights of 2-4 pounds in a year, 4-7 pounds in two years, and over 8 pounds in three years. They rarely live beyond three years, according to Capt. John Kowalczyk, out of Rochester, who claims their most common cause of death is over-eating.

Since the shoreline waters around the lake are rather shallow, direct sunlight warms them first. This warming continues rather slowly through the months of March and April, holding the brown trout in along the shoreline and up high in the water. Most of the fishing during these months takes place in this upper layer of warmer water, in fact usually in the upper five feet. Both lures and bait are used effectively.

It is not uncommon during this particular season to see small 14-foot boats catching large brown trout in the mouths of inlets leading to the lake. Although fishing out of a small boat on Lake Ontario isn't advisable, especially when the air temperature is hovering in the low 30's, many anglers still sneak out of the inlets into the main lake on extra calm days.

These small boats usually run flat lines off their transoms and use reels loaded with from 4-8 lb. test line. Often three to four rods will be used for trolling with some lures fished in near the boat, others dropped further back. Lures used include medium 3-4 inch swimming plugs such as Rebels, Rapalas, Baglies, Bombers, and Storm Lures. These long and thin baitfish imitations are trolled along with 2-3 inch spoons in the upper five feet of water.

Once a small boat has hooked into a large brown trout on light line, the fight is on! These fish quite often strike and then immediately leap out of the water. Sometimes, you see the fish leap or hear him splash before a rod is even tripped. This is because the brown will swim up behind the lure, putting on a burst of speed to overtake it, then, without putting any pressure on the rod jump up and out of the water. It is only when he reenters the water and streaks off in another direction that one of the rods will scream. This method, by the way, is called longlining, and in spring most longliners are successful!

OTHER SPECIES, TOO

Although some coho salmon, rainbow trout, landlocked salmon and lake trout show up in the early season catch, most anglers are really fishing for the more abundant browns. Remember, the rainbows are in the rivers still spawning while most cohos, landlocks and lake trout are offshore. Should these other species wander in along the beach, they respond well to the methods used for the browns. Keep in mind, then, that while we continue to talk about browns in this chapter, any of these other species could appear and respond to the methods described.

While some fishermen prefer using smaller boats with ultra light tackle, most anglers employ larger craft. The main advantage of a boat in excess of 20 feet is its ability to keep you sheltered from the weather while you're waiting for a fish to strike a trolled lure. When it is cold outside, when an even colder wind is blowing, when you are over 200 miles away from home, and when you decide to take a chance on the weather and go fishing, having the shelter of a big boat with a cabin can really save the day.

March is the coldest of the three ice-out months, and unless you are fishing some warm water discharge, you would probably be best advised to try and pick the warmest days.

From mid-April on, temperatures usually cooperate and the fishing conditions are even better on through the month of May. But don't let these months fool you! Although the weather appeared to be warming up, we were once caught out on the lake with Capt. John Kowalczyk in a blizzard during the third week of April. When the storm was finally over, the entire southern tier of the lake was covered with more than 25 inches of fresh fallen snow. If you plan a trip during this time period, be prepared for the worst and bring along some winter clothing. Foul weather gear is a must.

SIDE PLANER TACTICS

The best way to fish for ice-out species is with the aid of side planer boards (see Figs. 6-a,b,c). Very much like outriggers, the side planers take your lines and lures out away from the propeller turbulence created behind your boat. This is important when fishing shallow, since trout and in fact all salmonoid species tend to be shy and wary.

Each side planer board is attached to a cable and a reel. As the boat makes its way through the water, the cable is payed out and each board is deployed about 45 feet off a side gunnel at about a 50 degree angle to the side of the boat. Once the trolling speed is established, metal rings with rubber couplets or alligator clamps on their opposite ends are placed around the cables. A lure is dropped back some 25 feet off the transom of the boat, then the line from the lure is twisted some 3-5 times and placed between the rubber couplets (Jolly Release) or alligator clip (Laurvick, et al.). Now, the fishing reel that is attached to the lure being trolled is disengaged. Line is payed out until the ring is about 10 feet from the side planer placing the lure out some 35 feet from the prop turbulence. Three

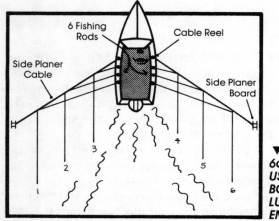

6a.
USING SIDE PLANER BOARDS TO GET LURES OUTSIDE ENGINE TURBULENCE

rods and lures are usually deployed in this manner in 10-foot increments.

It is always important to check the action of the lure before it is let down behind the boat, because every lure has a particular speed at which it operates best. To do so, set your speed at 2 MPH and run the lure off the side of the boat and back some 10 feet. Observe the lure's motion and adjust the speed of the boat to gain the lure's optimal action. Try not to go faster than 2¼ MPH during this early, inshore season. Also check the action of the lures from time to time while fishing. It only takes a small piece of weed or other debris to throw off their action.

Often after course changes, trollers fail to adjust their boat's speed. The result can be fewer if any strikes while trolling in the new direction. Why? Let's say you were trolling at optimal speed directly into the wind and catching fish. By changing course, you may now have the wind at your back. Even if you maintain the same engine RPM, your boat will be moving at a faster forward speed. Thus the lure action may no longer be ideal. What you must do at this point is check another lure behind the boat and readjust the boat's speed to accommodate the new course.

When a big brown trout decides to hit one of the lures behind the boat, he pulls the line free of its rubber couplet. The rod straightens up for a second or two, but as the fish gets in behind the transom, the rod will double over. Now is the time to strike the fish! Take the rod, reel to the fish (if necessary), and lift up on the rod, one time, very hard. Look at the reel. If the drag is giving and line is coming off, do not try to crank the handle. Wait until the line stops coming off the spool before trying to reel in the fish.

While all this is going on, keep the boat moving slowly forward. This will keep the fish from getting into the other lines and lures. If it's a really big fish, try to have someone reel in as many of the other lines, at least from one side of the boat, as possible.

If the fish makes a run at the boat, reel faster! Never allow the tip of your rod to slacken off. Your rod must always remain deeply bent. Keep even pressure on the fish. Eventually, he will tire and move in towards the boat. At this time, get a big net ready. When the fish is spent and at the side of the boat, place the net under him and lift him up quickly into the boat.

Many fish are lost just before they are netted. One of the chief reasons is that anglers get a look at what they are fighting and try to speed up the landing process by doing something foolish like putting their thumb on the spool to drag the fish forward. This accomplishes one of two things: the extra pressure alerts the fish of danger and he makes one last ditch effort to escape; or, the extra pressure of the thumb causes either the line to break or the lure to pull free. Sometimes, the free flying lure injures the angler waiting to net the fish. The moral is to try and remain cool while boating any fish. Take your time and by all means let your tackle do the work.

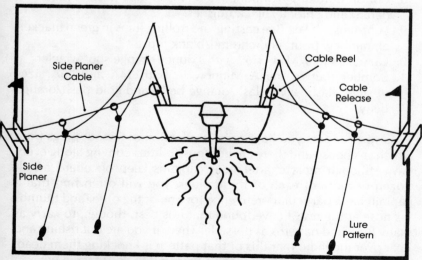

▶ 6b. USING SIDE PLANERS — Rear View

AN ICE-OUT LURE SELECTION

There are many lures on the market today that will effectively catch ice-out brown trout and other species that are in close feeding on the spawning baitfish. Most of these lures are long and thin and many are imitations of smelt, perch, or alewife "moon-eye" herring. Although it is impossible to name all the lures on the market, here are some that have been among the most consistent producers:

1. Rebel Minnows with the silver/black, gold/black, gold/orange back, rainbow trout, and fluorescent red finishes in sizes #11 and 13.
2. Storm Lure's Little Mac and Shallomac in silver and green finishes.
3. Mann's 3/8-ounce Shad-Mann and 1/4-ounce Razorback Pig in green and red dot chartreuse patterns.
4. Smithwick's Rouge Shallow Diver 1/3-ounce in perch finish.
5. Rapala's original floater in flourescent red, chartreuse diamond, black/silver, and gold/silver patterns in size #11 (both one piece and jointed).
6. Bagley's Bang-O-Lure 4¼'' series in orange/gold and green/chartreuse on silver.
7. Heddon's Tadpolly and River Runt in XRY and RFB color patterns.
8. Cotton Cordell's ⅜th ounce Red Fins in mackerel (looks like a perch) and chrome/black finishes.
9. Luhr-Jensen's Sea-Bee casting and trolling lures in green mackerel, rainbow trout, and chrome/black top.
10. Lazy Ike's KL4/M14, 3½'' ⅝th's ounce orange spot wiggler.
11. Bomber Bait's Long A Minnow in both 14A and 15A sizes in silver flash, silver flash/orange belly, and gold flash/orange belly.

As you can see, you have quite a selection of ice-out plugs from which to choose and there are new possibilities coming along every day. Although most charter boat captains keep on board a half dozen or more of each of these plugs, you will often find that a captain has a particular preference for one or the other and thumbs his nose at the rest. I have found that it is best, though, to carry as many lures and patterns as possible. Then, if you are out fishing and hear over the radio that this or that pattern is knocking them dead, you will at least stand a chance of having it in your tackle box.

By the way, there are two tackle boxes that seem especially well designed to accommodate the types of lures and tackle used on Lake Ontario. These are the Plano 757 and the Fenwick 35.1 Drawer Boxes. Both boxes have large compartments, and lures stored within them are easy to find and access.

Other lures are effective on the ice-out species and these consist primarily of spoons and flutter spoons. The hot colors for these lures again bear much resemblance to the forage species available at this time. Dark and light green, blue, silver, red streaked, and gold represent the productive colors.

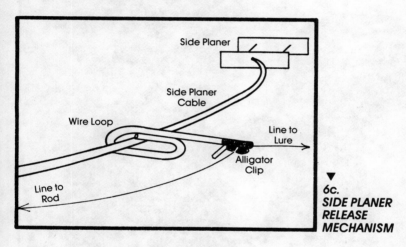

Side Planer

Side Planer Cable

Wire Loop

Line to Lure

Alligator Clip

Line to Rod

▼
**6c.
SIDE PLANER
RELEASE
MECHANISM**

Trolling strategies for this time of year are fairly basic. Fish most or all lures in the upper stratum of water, making certain they're performing properly, and keep all lures out of the prop turbulence. If you follow just these simple instructions, you should have few problems catching fish. However, there are some tricks that will help you totally utilize the level of water you are fishing and up the odds of catching a giant brown trout.

You can use the following devices if you have them: a fish finder, a downrigger, and a surface temperature gauge. However, during ice-out fishing, these devices aren't necessary to make limit catches of fish. For one thing, since the fish are up high in the water, and since they run from prop turbulence, it will be hard to read them on a fish finder. Also, since you are fishing in the upper 5 feet or so of water, most of the lures will get down the required distance, foregoing the need for a downrigger. And since the water temperature all along the shoreline and in the bays is acceptable and fairly uniform (not optimal but warmer than the rest of the lake), a surface temperature recorder isn't strictly needed either. Nonetheless, if you want to catch lunker browns in excess of 10 pounds, you just might want to employ some of these devices at least some of the time.

TROPHY STRATEGIES

Brown trout have a strong tendency to remain near the bottom much of the time, but large browns have a tendency to stay down even in the early season. Tactics for truly large browns, then, are somewhat different. Let's say, for example, that you are fishing in 12 feet of water and are bringing your lures through the upper five feet or so. It is advisable to keep a fish finder on to look for large blips on or very near the bottom. If you get some, then use a downrigger to get a lure about a foot or two above the bottom. Set the downrigger at nine feet and allow the lure to swim down perhaps a foot or two.

Big brown trout are not only loners, they are also very boat shy. You may have to run lures intended for them 60-100 feet behind the boat. Another trait of big browns is that they will seldom chase a lure. They want to be able to grab it as it slowly passes by. If the lure is too fast, the big fish will not bite! So, watch your forward speed. This is a critical factor for catching larger fish in colder water this early in the year.

Some places to look for really big fish are in bays or river mouths and near warm water discharges. There are many bays, some of the better ones being near Rochester, Sodus Point, Oswego, and the large Bay of Mexico. Big browns come from such places as the Niagara River, Eighteen Mile Creek, Braddocks Bay, Irondequoit Bay, Sodus Bay, Port Bay, Little Sodus Bay, the Oswego Bay (inside the break walls) and River, and off Nine Mile Island in the Bay of Mexico.

If the main lake is too rough due to wind or storm conditions, some of these backwaters offer protection and opportunity. Relatively shallow, these extensions of the lake warm quickly and house sizable populations of brown trout early in the spring. If a storm is severe enough, it may also drive jack coho salmon into the inlets of these protected harbors where they will be caught along with the browns. At times like these, fish mud lines. A mud line is where the warmer muddy water from the creek and stream runoff (due to the storm) enters the lake. Cohos and browns are often found in this warmer muddy water from where they may dart out and strike passing lures.

SPECIFIC FISHING LOCATIONS

Fishing near a power plant that releases warm water into the lake improves your chances of catching browns. The warm water increases the trout's metabolism, and rather than having to hang around the bottom until the water warms up, even the bigger browns chase lures. The power plants discharging warm water into the lake are: the Nine Mile Island Nuclear Power Plant in the Bay of Mexico between the Salmon River mouth and Oswego; the Oswego Station; the R.E. Ginna Nuclear Power Plant between Webster and Sodus Point; Russell Station west of Rochester; and the Somerset Power Plant located east of the Niagara River's entrance to Lake Ontario. Fishing for ice-out species at these locations means dragging your lures through the area where the warm water is entering the lake.

These warm waters attract a great many fishermen. Since many boats fish the same general location, a trolling pattern develops that (hopefully) accommodates everyone. The pattern consists of boats fishing in a big circle giving each boat the opportunity to swing through the warm water discharge and hook up. Whether a boat hooks up or not, it must stay in the circle and wait its turn to swing back through the warm water. If it does hook up, it continues moving in the circle while fighting the fish. Eventually, while continuing in the circle, it will reach the warm water again and be given another opportunity to catch the feeding trout.

Other good locations are in front of the inlets and creeks (remember, fish the muddy water if it's available). These waters coming from inland are warmer than the lake proper, and cause big fish to remain, warm up, and feed. It isn't uncommon to see many boats early in the morning trolling outside an inlet.

Although it can be done, baitfishing these early browns is generally unproductive. The air and water temperatures remain so cold that fish are sluggish and trolling is far more effective. Later on in the year, many popular bait fishing methods can be put to work and we'll discuss these in some of the following chapters.

SPRING TROLLING

"As spring advances, the weather improves: Blizzards become less likely. But the one nice day in seven can mean bruiser browns, sleek lakers and feisty football cohos."

Lake Ontario is such a large lake that conditions will vary from place to place. For example, conditions that exist at one spot may prevail a week later in a locale that is slightly colder. So, as we discuss a particular season, understand that each location around the lake has its own seasonal schedule and that what is being presented here is a good general outline of the various possible seasons and fishing opportunitites. All will have to be slightly adjusted to reflect any one specific location.

As spring advances, the weather improves: Blizzards become less likely. But the one nice day in seven can mean bruiser browns, sleek lakers and feisty football cohos. It is now as spring trolling starts that ice-out fishing ends. This new season, along with its different tactics, is characterized by what is called a spring turn-over. The turn-over refers to a physical change in the water itself. It occurs when the relatively narrow band of cold surface water begins to warm and equalize in density with the warmer less dense water below (much of that lower water stratum may be below 39 degrees Fahrenheit — maximum density for water). Helped by wind action, this warmed and increasingly dense surface water begins to sink to the bottom. The less dense colder water on the bottom begins to rise to the surface and the water actually "turns-over." Sometimes you can see this happen. It becomes evident, for example, when the lighter, less dense water rises and brings bottom algae up to the surface in the shallower portions of the lake. A visible green film develops and spreads out evenly on the surface giving the lake an appearance of being covered with green dust.

While this is going on, the primary species inshore remain pretty much the same. Fishermen attempt to catch brown trout, rainbow trout (domestic and steelhead), lake trout, and an occasional salmon. The size of the fish remains for trout from 3-15 pounds and salmon from 3-6 pounds. Browns still dominate fish catch totals with lake trout beginning to come on strong.

A DIFFICULT TIME OF YEAR
However, during this turn-over or spring trolling season, fishing becomes more difficult. Since there aren't yet any distinct temperature layers, the fish spread out from the top of the lake to the bottom and become less concentrated everywhere. During this short season, the great limit catches of five fish per angler per

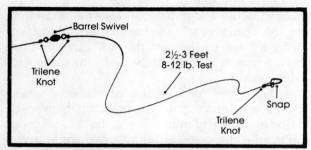

▶ *7a. TROLLING LEADER — A trolling leader should be used between the terminal end of your line and your lure. It prevents twisting and allows you to use lighter line.*

day made during ice-out decline, and a good catch now consists of one or two fish per angler.

The best thing about this season is that it only lasts for a short period of time, perhaps two weeks or less. To try and pin-point its exact occurrence is impossible, but it will happen annually some-time between the latter part of April and the beginning of June. Even though the lake turns over and fishing success decreases, there are certain things you can do to help maximize your score.

One clever evasive tactic is to simply find a section of lake that isn't presently being affected by the turn-over (since, as mentioned, one location may be in turn-over and another section still in ice-out). As an illustration, it seems that the southern tier area between the Niagara River and Oswego turns over before that area between Oswego and the Salmon River (Mexico Bay). If you can, trailer your boat to an area where the fishing is presently hot! If you can't, then understand why the fishing may be slacking off and try to make the most of it.

WHERE TO RIDE IT OUT
During turn-over is when a good captain earns his reputation. He must be able to locate and troll near various fish-holding structures, and then he must be able to persist in showing his lures to the spread of fish until they are ready to feed. The good captain looks for deep drop-offs, irregular bottom features, sand bars, shallow underwater islands, irregular shorelines, thermal bars (to be discussed in the

next chapter) and inlets. Any one of these features may hold a sizable population of gamefish and it may only be a matter of time until they get over the changing temperature patterns and feed. Even if you can locate the fish though, use the right lures, and fish hard you'll still find the turn-over period to be a waiting game with action intermittent at best.

A fish finder really helps here. With it, at least you know where the fish are. If they aren't biting, you can mark their presence and then go try to find another structure that may hold more cooperative fish. If you're still unsuccessful return to where you previously marked fish on your recorder and see if they have started feeding yet.

You will not need to travel too far offshore to find the types of structures named or the fish concentrated there. The depth should be less than 100 feet of water, and this will usually keep you well within a mile of the shoreline.

One of the best places to find fish during the turn-over period is near river mouths or inlets. Here again, warmer water is entering, and the water may remain warm in the inlet area and even out into the main lake. This is temperature-stable water, and the gamefish readily respond by feeding in it. Even knowing that inlets or openings between the main lake and bay are prime fish attractors, your next problem becomes which inlet or bay is going to hold fish? If you do not have a reliable source of information, such as a tackle shop or charter boat captain, then you must fish by trial and error. You should also keep an ever tuned ear to the VHF radio and listen for someone who might indicate where fish are cooperating.

The second most stable location is near warm water discharges. While they, too, offer up poorer catches during the turn-over season, you should still be able to manage a fish or two. Run lures at the depth fish are shown on the recorder. If the fish seem to be spread out from the top to the bottom, vertically spread your lures.

Another thing that you should keep alert for is a "herring" or "gull" line. For some reason, anywhere warm water meets cold during this early season, dead or dying herring accumulate and are visible in a slick running in a straight line along the surface. Gulls, often attracted by the lure of an easy meal, give the presence of the line and warmer water away. By fishing this mix you may find trout in the warmer water just waiting for an easy meal to pass by.

Sand bars, underwater high areas or islands, and irregular land

Most people have never seen, let alone caught a 20-pound brown. This gorgeous fish is evidence that Lake Ontario can offer up world class fish.

features equate to havens for the fish and help you wait out the turn-over period. Gamefish on these structures are sometimes finicky about taking lures, but it's worth trying for them anyway.

KEY BOTTOM STRUCTURES

Rough bottom and deep drop-offs offer other stable areas where baitfish can hide from their attackers. By finding such underwater structures, you should be able to locate some fish. The best way is with a topographic map, a fish finder, and much experience. The best topographic map series of the lake is the U.S. Department of Commerce Loran-C Overprinted 14803 through 14806. You can purchase these maps from the DEC in Washington, D.C. or in some marinas around the lake.

On any topographic map, contour lines merging together and narrowly separated depict steep, underwater drop-offs or cliffs. Although there are actually few such locations along Ontario's shoreline, some deep drop-offs are associated with inlets. Often, water rushing out of inlets during stormy weather creates long, deep furrows which extend out for some distance into the lake. Should you cross one of these troughs while trolling along the coast, it would register as a steep drop-off on your recorder. Such bottom features are not always indicated on topographic maps. This is because they are not part of the fixed geography, but rather may occur from time to time or storm to storm. You must search them out and utilize the stable water temperatures around them to find fish.

Several other species besides the brown trout become active during this season. For example, the coho, domestic rainbow, and steelhead all begin to show up more consistently in fish catches. Not being bottom huggers like the browns, these fish have remained offshore where they often feed within 10 feet of the surface near thermal bars. As the bars begin to blend with the warming surface waters, many of these other fish tend to move inshore and become more available. It is only during the mid to late spring period that all these species can be caught inshore in the same level or stratum of water at the same time.

Tackle requirements for all these spring species are the same, namely trolling outfits, side planer boards and/or downriggers. But, besides the addition of downriggers, tackle can change somewhat from what is used during ice-out. For example, since the fish will be spread out more from top to bottom, diving lures can be substituted for the floating lures used almost exclusively during the ice-out season. Still, leave a few floaters in your arsenal because at this volatile time or year you really never know when or where the fish are going to cooperate.

"Let's leave two lures off each board," called Captain Ron Clark to Ray Finney who was acting as mate. "Make one a floater and the other a sinker. We should also run some spoons down on the riggers. Put them around 15, 25, and 40 feet deep. There are plenty of good marks showing in that region on the recorder."

Ray followed the captain's instructions and soon we were pulling eight lures through the various strata of water from the surface down to about 40 feet.

"There's one on," called Mike Kersey, as he reached for the rod that had straightened up in the left rod holder. No sooner did he get the rod in hand when up and out of the water came his magnificent fish. It had struck a size #11 flourescent red, floating Rebel Jointed-Minnow.

"He's really pulling off line," added Mike, "Now he's headed right for the boat!"

As the big fish neared the boat, he came out of the water again, almost as if trying to see who was annoying him.

"It's a brown," came the simultaneous reply! And what a brown it was, almost 10 pounds!

Yes, this was during the slow turn-over season, but expertise and an effective trolling pattern had quickly brought favorable results. A good trolling pattern during this turn-over season should have from six to eight rods working with up to 12 lures spread out evenly from the surface down to over 40 feet. Find the fish and keep at them until you can see some catch pattern developing. That is, are all the fish coming from a particular level? If they are, get more lures to that level. If the strikes remain spread out and no pattern becomes evident, as usually occurs during this period, then keep the lures spread out and keep picking away at the spread out fish.

COHO — AVAILABLE AND EDIBLE

The yearling coho salmon, which are caught inshore during this time, range in weight from 2-6 pounds. Cohos are often called "silver salmon," but both names refer to the exact same fish. Anglers are often confused about this. These beautiful members of the salmon family are long and sleek, capable of great bursts of speed and good pressure. Sometimes they will become airborne leapers, clearing the surface of the water. But, during the early spring season, a bulldogging fight much like that of a large bass is to be expected. What's best is that jack (small yearling) cohos under 21 inches are deemed perfectly safe to eat.

The domestic rainbow trout and steelhead are biologically the very same species (Salmo gairdneri) but possess different body builds, fighting abilities, and most importantly, migratory habits.

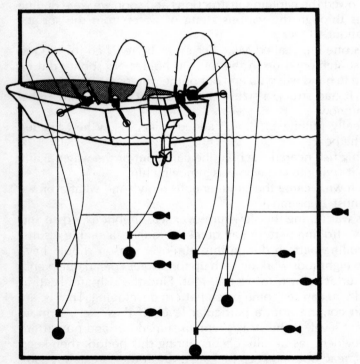

▶ *7b. DOWNRIGGER LURE SPREAD PATTERN — Downrigger patterns can be most complex! Here, eight lures are deployed on six rods. Stacking systems make it possible (drawing is intentionally out of perspective for illustrative purposes).*

The steelhead, which is technically a strain of rainbow, is the stronger of the two and most times the larger. A good size steelhead may go 18 pounds, while a good sized domestic might top the scale at around 10 pounds. However, during the early spring season, both of these fish will average generally in the neighborhood of 6-8 pounds.

A typical steelhead strike often sees the rod tip diving for the water, while the big, sleek, beautiful fish comes straight up and out of the water buzz-saw style. It will often make many leaps in rapid succession. Once back under the water, the big fish will swim off in a drag testing direction before tiring and coming to net.

As for the more docile domestic rainbow, it will tire quickly after a relatively lackluster fight. However, what the bow fails to deliver in fighting spirit, it makes up for in beauty. These are big, broad, colorful fish, some with a handsome red streak running along their lateral line. The domestic rainbow also has many dark spots all over its body and caudal (tail) fin, making it truly worth mounting. The steelhead, on the other hand, displays a greenish black dorsal (top) section with a silvery white side and bottom.

Soon after the turn-over season passes, stratification occurs, the thermocline forms and fishing improves. This thermal stratification gives way to a whole new type of fishing which is referred to as the late spring trolling and baitfishing season covered in the next chapter.

LATE SPRING TROLLING AND BAIT FISHING

*"If you can find the magical
edge of a thermal barrier,
you may find steelhead, cohos
and rainbows stacked up like
cordwood."*

8

Whereas spring trolling is difficult and unstable, late spring trolling regains stability. This reversal comes about after the spring turnover, discussed in the previous chapter. After this turnover, distinct layers or "temperature zones" are formed. Eventually, the top warm water is separated from the deep cold water by a buffer zone called the "thermocline" or zone of greatest temperature change (technically where the water drops 1.8 degrees Fahrenheit for every 3.28 feet of depth). In early spring, the water was cold everywhere, but now fish can seek and find the exact water temperature they prefer.

Water on the bottom will be cold, while various strata of water temperatures will be encountered as one ascends. Each gamefish, including trout and salmon, shows a distinct preference for a particular temperature. And although a fish certainly will leave its temperature zone at times (i.e. to chase baitfish), if you locate a preferred temperature you have greatly increased your chances of locating a particular gamefish.

UNDERSTANDING STRATIFICATION

Inshore during late spring, or when the thermocline first develops, you might find surface water temperatures reaching 70 degrees (within a mile of shore; offshore the surface is much colder). Down, say, 10 feet, the temperature might be around 60 degrees. This 60-degree water layer may occupy the next ten feet, with this ten-foot zone forming the bottom part of the thermocline. Below this, water temperature will drop until the water reaches its densest at 39.2 degrees F.

Let's say you encounter this hypothetical scenario and are interested in catching brown trout. The brown's ideal temperature is somewhere around 60 degrees, so you should simply troll, or fish bait between 10-20 feet (see Fig. 8-a). As the season progresses and the days get hotter, the warmer water on the surface will push the thermocline deeper. Therefore, temperature readings taken on a daily basis are recommended to establish the depth and extent of the thermocline. It should be noted that, at this time, a gamefish's preferred temperature will not *always* fall within the thermocline, but it sometimes will. This is most true with browns.

Early most mornings, while people are getting their baits and lures into the water, captains talk to each other and share information concerning the various temperatures they have encountered. They cross reference information and try to stay on top of the temperature and depth situation in the area in which they are fishing.

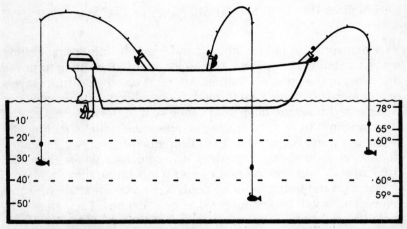

▶ 8a. TEMPERATURE FISHING WITH BAIT — Vertically place baits through the level showing the preferred temperature for the species you seek. Important: Sometimes you must find where a preferred temperature meets bottom. At other times gamefish will be suspended in their temperature zone.

FINDING THE RIGHT TEMPERATURE

Water temperature can be recorded on several kinds of devices. These can be as simple as a thermometer on the end of a line. Simply drop to the desired depth, pull back up quickly and read what it says. However, be aware that an ordinary thermometer used in this manner will not be extremely accurate for either temperature or depth.

For a little more money, you can buy a hand held thermometer, like the Lowrence Electronics Fish-N-Temp. This device has a dial face and a length of cable calibrated at one foot intervals with a thermal couplet on the end. The thermal couplet is lowered into the water where it sends back the temperature to the dial, while the depth of the couplet is shown right on the calibrated cable itself (see Fig. 8-b).

For still a few bucks more, you can buy a downrigger with a thermal couplet and depth gauge all in one. Now, as you lower your lures you can read the temperature at various depths.

For some species, you will have to fish deeper than for browns. Lakers prefer 51 degrees, salmon 53-55 degrees, while rainbows, steelhead in particular, are fond of 54-56 degrees. So, as stated above, find a particular temperature stratum and an associated species should become catchable.

THERMAL BARS

Besides the thermocline, in May and June another significant water temperature formation develops from 4-6 miles off the southern tier. It is called a "thermal bar" or "thermal barrier" (see Fig. 8-c). Water temperatures drop sharply all along its edge at the surface until the densest water at 39.2 degrees F. is reached. This zone attracts rainbow trout and some coho salmon which follow the bar as it slowly moves offshore.

If you find the magical edge of a thermal barrier — a thermocline bent upwards — you may find steelhead, cohos and domestic rainbows stacked up like cordwood.

The bars are formed when colder layers of water found beneath the thermocline inshore actually bend up well offshore and come close to if not touch the surface. Rainbow trout and coho salmon like these conditions and feed within the upper stratum of water. As the inshore water warms and pushes the bars further offshore, both these species follow. Eventually, the surface warms all over, and the thermal bars disappear.

One year, while fishing with Capt. Ed Dorscheid of C-Frog Charters

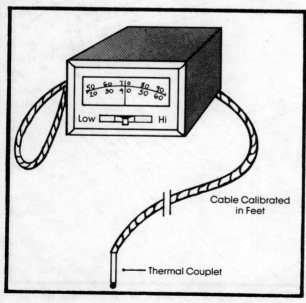

Cable Calibrated in Feet

Thermal Couplet

▼
8b.
USING A
THERMAL
PROBE

Lower the thermal couplet. Read the water temperature on the dial and the depth on the calibrated cable.

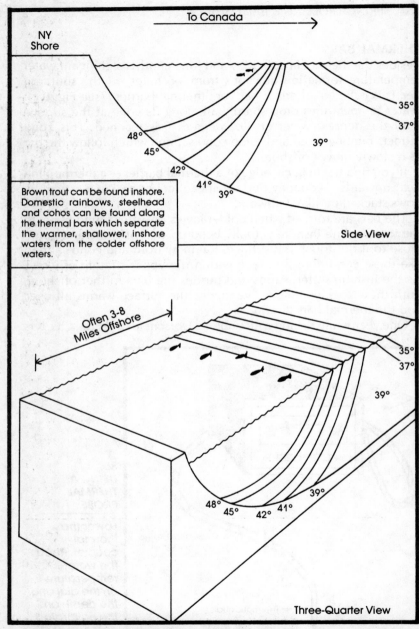

To Canada →

NY Shore

35°
37°
39°
48°
45°
42°
41°
39°

Brown trout can be found inshore. Domestic rainbows, steelhead and cohos can be found along the thermal bars which separate the warmer, shallower, inshore waters from the colder offshore waters.

Side View

Often 3-8 Miles Offshore

35°
37°
39°
48°
45°
42°
41°
39°

Three-Quarter View

▶ 8c¹. *SIMPLIFIED EARLY THERMAL BAR FORMATION — A general spring temperature profile of water along the southern tier.*

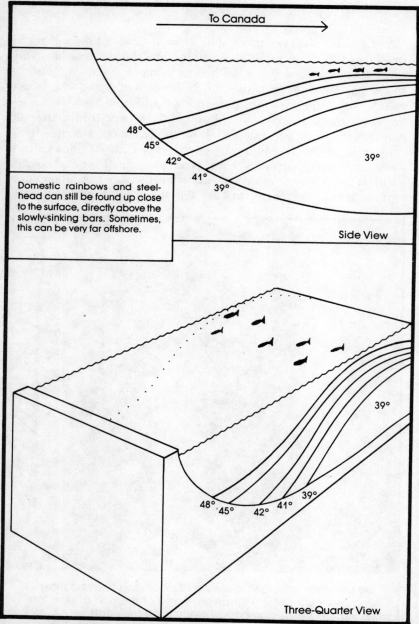

To Canada →

48°
45°
42°
41°
39°

39°

Domestic rainbows and steelhead can still be found up close to the surface, directly above the slowly-sinking bars. Sometimes, this can be very far offshore.

Side View

39°

48° 45° 42° 41° 39°

39°

Three-Quarter View

▶ 8c². *LATE SPRING THERMAL BAR—Theoretically, the thermal bars disappear when all the surface water has risen above 39 F., usually some time in June.*

out of Sodus Point, we encountered many excellent days of prime steelhead fishing in close association with the thermal bars four miles straight out of Sodus. Ed had us using Luhr Jensen Hotshots and small Wobble Troll lures in flourescent red and chartreuse colors. He would put them 10 feet down and from 10-30 feet back on downriggers. Then, he would troll in the vicinity of the thermal bars and the result was fine action on the tenacious steelhead!

In spite of the serendipitous encounters with steelhead, from early June into August most trout taken are pale green and possess a forked tail. This not so mysterious fish is the lake trout, an important summertime species in Lake Ontario. Lake trout are usually

▶ *Big domestic rainbows, cohos and steelhead (this is a steelie) can be caught at the landward edge of thermal bars in late spring. One especially good place is off of Olcott.*

structure fish. In order to catch them, lures should be fished in 51 degrees of water and in close proximity to some bottom structure. Combine these two components and you are in business.

As the season progresses, the lake trout move further offshore and deeper following the 51 degree water temperature level. They rarely rise much off the bottom, except when the 51-degree mark gets too deep. This is discussed further in Ch. 12.

WHERE TO FISH

One terrific location for lunker lakers is off Stony Point Lighthouse near Henderson Harbor. This is below the entrance to the St. Lawrence Seaway and the Thousand Island section in the upper northeast corner of Ontario. During the month of June, 51 degrees of water is usually found down between 60-100 feet. This coincides beautifully with the underwater canyons and steep drop-offs which offer much protection for both the bait and lakers found there. In order to fish this location, downriggers, thermometers, plugs, spoons, and a real good fish finder unit should be used.

Not only must a fish finder find fish, but it must also be able to accurately display a detailed line or picture of the bottom. This is necessary to allow you time to adjust downriggers whenever the bottom fails to cooperate. For example, suppose you are trolling and you have three downriggers about 80 feet deep. Then, all of a sudden, the fish finder indicates that the bottom (which has been showing 95 feet down or so) is coming up. If the bottom comes up to above the 80 foot mark before you have the opportunity to adjust the downriggers, all three rigs may get hung up on the bottom. Thus, the fish finder is extremely important. It not only finds fish, but also indicates precisely where the bottom is and when the depth is changing.

Anglers have devised many different ways to seduce lake trout and we'll discuss each one now in as much detail as space permits. There are three general categories: trolling (trolling sinkers, wire line, lead core line, planers, and downriggers), jigging (copper line and monofilament line), and baitfishing.

TROLLING

While trolling, there are many ways to get your lures down to the fish. One includes using a heavy weight or trolling sinker 6-8 feet in front of the lures. This catches fish but as the weight (which may average from 6-10 ounces) increases, its effectiveness decreases. Tackle becomes heavy and you're never really quite sure of exactly how deep your lures are. Still, this process can be used to get your lures down 50 feet or more. Just attach the trolling sinker to the end of your line, add about a 6-8 foot leader, run your lure on a snap off the end, then position your rod in the stern of the boat.

Sometimes, this method is called "flat line trolling." Actually, flat line trollers sometimes use no weight at all. The no-weight method is effective in only the upper 15 feet. Weight or no weight, though, when the 51 degree water temperature needed to catch lake trout gets down beneath 25 feet, you have the old problem of never really knowing exactly how deep your lures are. Let out too much line and you're on the bottom, don't let out enough or have too light a trolling sinker, and you're above the fish. Thus even though flat line trolling is an acceptable practice during the ice-out season when fish are up high, once the thermocline begins to form other means must be used to take lakers consistently.

This is when wire and lead core lines come into play. Once the only real way to effectively troll in deep water, these techniques lost many devotees because of the cumbersomeness of the operation. You need big reels and strong rods — two components which truly overmatch the poor fighting qualities of the lake trout.

Wire and lead core line can be used comfortably to fish as deep as 45 feet. Deeper than that, you have to use too much line to make it much fun. As a rule of thumb, you can get down from 5-7 feet per 50 feet of wire depending upon the forward speed of the boat. In order to get down 45 feet, you will need 300 feet of wire, which is not very sporting because when a fish bites, all you feel on the other end is a heavy weight. Trolling sinkers can be added to increase the depth per length of line out.

Lead core line is very bulky. In order to use 300 feet, you would have to use a much larger reel. Once the entire outfit (reel, rod, and line) gets too heavy, the sport of fighting the fish is lost. However, if you want to use one of these methods, run your wire or lead core line out and attach a lure to the end of a 15-20 foot leader. To get down even deeper, add a trolling weight at the end of the line 6-8 feet in front of the lure or use a diving plug with or without the weight.

Not too long ago, planers came on the scene and they are still in

force today. A planer device (there are many different types) is a
piece of metal or plastic that, when pulled through the water behind
the boat, goes down deep pulling a lure along 6-8 feet behind it.
This is not to be confused with the "side planers" discussed in
previous chapters. Once the fish strikes the lure, the device col-
lapses and is supposed to offer no resistence. We have used Luhr
Jensen's Dipsy Divers effectively to get our lures down as deep as
70 feet or more. Again, though, there is the serious problem of
never really knowing exactly how deep your lures are.

Next on the scene came the downrigger (to be discussed briefly
here and then in greater detail in Ch. 11). With this device, an
angler can run any lure down to any depth and be sure it will *stay*
at that depth (see Figs. 8-d,e). A downrigger is actually a pulley

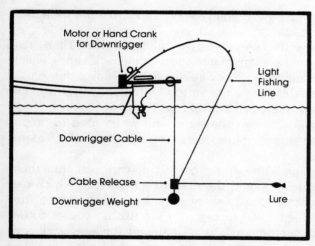

▼
8d.
**BASIC
DOWNRIGGER
SYSTEM**
**Lower the
cannonball
(downrigger
weight) to the
proper depth
and troll.**

Motor or Hand Crank
for Downrigger

Light
Fishing
Line

Downrigger Cable

Cable Release

Downrigger Weight

Lure

system consisting of a cable to which is attached a heavy weight.
On that same cable, just above the weight, is a snap device called a
"release mechanism." The line from a fishing rod is attached to this
snap, and when a fish strikes the lure, the line snaps off the device
and you fight the fish without any other encumberances on your
line. Most downriggers come with digital counters which record
the exact depth of the lures, and a thermal couplet which measures
the exact water temperature at that depth.

Several lures have proven effective on June lake trout. Storm

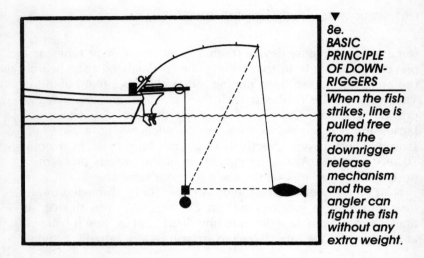

▼
8e.
BASIC PRINCIPLE OF DOWNRIGGERS
When the fish strikes, line is pulled free from the downrigger release mechanism and the angler can fight the fish without any extra weight.

Lure's ThinFin, Wiggle Wart, and Wee Wart all have enticing action and fish catching abilities. The Alpena Diamond and Little Cleo manufactured by Acme Lures are also excellent choices. Then there are Mann's chartreuse Finn Mann and Hackleback series which have proven themselves on a day in, day out basis over the years.

Other well-tested lures are the Sutton Flutter spoon series, Pine Valley Flutter spoons, the Evil Eye, and the Westport Wobbler. These lures actually swim through the water and when used in proper combination with attracting lures like Mann's Chartreuse Finn Mann are quite deadly.

To troll these lures effectively behind downriggers, run them back from 10-60 feet behind the downrigger weights, which can also work as attractors. Start fishing some lures back 10 feet. Run others back between 15-30 feet. If you see fish on your recorder and can't seem to get them to bite, start moving the lures back until strikes are registered. If no strikes come, drop the lures back some more, but not further than 60 feet.

Another thing you can do is adjust the speed of your boat. Lake trout require a very slow forward speed. Try to keep it under 2 MPH and still assure the proper lure action before lowering the weights to the proper temperature (51 degrees in this case) and depth. Some boats have a difficult time operating at such a low RPM. If this is the case with your boat, try running sea anchors off each gunwale. They will allow you to run at higher RPM, yet effectively decrease your forward speed. Now, with the lures running at the proper speed behind the downrigger weights, they should quickly gain attention. Spread the downrigger weights to cover the 51 degree water temperature range and troll the lures near the bottom or just above some structure.

"All the lures are 60 to 90 feet down," Mike Kersey said. "The 90-foot rigger is in 50 degrees of water and the 60-foot is in 52 degrees. The other two are in 51 degrees and are down 70 and 80 feet. Remember, the left rigger is highest . . . the right one is the lowest, so if we have to bring them up fast because of an irregular bottom, start with the right downrigger first," Mike instructed.

It wasn't long before the right middle downrigger rod snapped up!

"Fish on," Mike called as I grabbed for the upright rod. Reeling to the fish, I can remember saying, "you should have seen the mark this fish made on the screen! It is either a big laker or a submarine."

After striking, my big 9 foot rod bent deeply toward the water. One minute went by, then another. Soon, though, the big fish began to tire, and yielding to the rod pressure, slowly rose towards the surface.

"There he is," I yelled, while Mike readied the big net.

"You weren't whistling Dixie, this is a big one!" came Mike's reply as he scooped up the 13 pound plus lake trout.

The dandy forktail had fallen for a Sutton "88" Spoon fished slowly 20 feet behind the 80 foot deep downrigger weight offshore of Stony Point near Henderson Harbor.

"Keep track of the next hit," requested Captain Ron Clark, "and if it comes from that depth again, raise the 90 footer and lower the 60."

Trolling with downriggers during this season can produce explosive results. Downriggers keep the lures at the exact depth and temperature you desire, and they also allow you to move things around in an effort to improve your catch. Perhaps most important of all, they let you fight the fish without extra weight or heavy line. Unlike virtually every other deep-water technique, downrigger fishing truly allows you to enjoy the fish and its natural fighting ability.

How many fish might you expect to catch on a June trip? My friend Ron Jacobsen supplied me with the following account of a trip with three buddies and Capt. Paul Lewandowski, on the Trophy Hunter out of Sodus Bay. Ron said that the group hooked 21 fish and boated 18. The total catch included 8 steelhead, 7 lakers, one rainbow, one chinook salmon, and one coho salmon.

A rare day? Not really. At the exact same time, I was fishing with several friends and Capt. Ron Clark as partially described above, out of North "Sandy" Pond above the Salmon River, in the vicinity

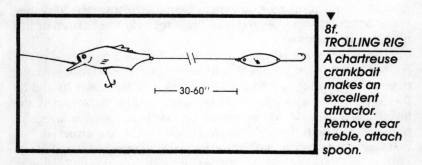

▼
8f.
TROLLING RIG
A chartreuse crankbait makes an excellent attractor. Remove rear treble, attach spoon.

30-60''

of Stony Point (this is the northern tier as opposed to Sodus Bay which is southern tier). We caught our limit of lake trout, 12 in all to 13½ pounds and 8 browns between 4 and 8 pounds. Yes, June is a very fine month to be out on Lake Ontario.

JIGGING
The second main method you might opt for during this period is jigging. There are two styles of jigging: "copper line" and "monofilament line." Although we don't really advocate the use of copper line, you might be interested to know something about it.

While jigging with copper line, you shouldn't be in water over 100 feet deep. A flat, sandy bottom is preferred, and you should have a copper line rod and reel which is much shorter and sturdier than other, more conventional outfits. Attach a 15-foot monofilament leader to a barrel swivel at the end of the copper line. Place a snap at the other end and add a lure. Typically, lures are 3-5 inch silver spoons, some with blue streaks through them like the Evil Eye. Lake trout are the primary targets.

Run the copper line out until it comes in contact with the bottom. Now, put the rod and reel down. Grab the copper line in your bare or gloved hand and point your hand down at the lure. Once the slack in the line has been taken up by the drift, pull it up to a point above your head. If you're doing things correctly, you should feel two distinct bumps at the other end of the line. The first bump is the copper coming off the bottom and the second bump is the lure following it.

Should you not feel two distinct bumps, you either have too much line on the bottom, indicating you should take up some

slack, or your line isn't in contact with the bottom, wherein you must let out more line. After making the required adjustments, pull away again. When two bumps are felt, continue lifting and dropping the lure until a fish strikes. Once the laker strikes, you must hook him with a pull of your hand, while reaching for the rod and reel. Then, while not allowing the fish any slack, reel him in.

Sound difficult? It is, and while it is an old and venerable method, it is now used by very few fishermen on Lake Ontario.

For jigging with monofilament line, bucktail jigs ranging in weight from ½ - 2 ounces are the popular lures. Always attempt to fish the lightest bucktail possible. However deeper water, stronger current, and more intense wind will all dictate the actual weight required. Should conditions mandate a bucktail in excess of 2 ounces, abandon the technique and go back to one of the others.

Bucktails work best when fished with an attached hook, rather than a free swinging hook. White or yellow or a combination of the two have been most successful. Instead of bucktails, heavy spoons like the Alpena Diamond, Little Cleo, Krocodile, Kastmaster, and Hopkins can be used. Stick to either solid gold and silver colors or silver/blue combinations when using these spoons.

One modification that you might consider making to these spoons is the substitution of a single, sturdy, size #5/0 nickle Siwash or salmon hook for the trebles. The single hook not only gives the lure a good side-to-side swagger, it also makes it difficult for the fish to get off the hook.

Now, as an added inducement place a piece of filleted creek chub or river sucker on the jig or spoon. You will increase its overall effectiveness tenfold! Although it is doubtful that you can buy this bait, chubs or suckers can be caught days ahead of your trip, filleted, cut into tapered strips (3-4 inches long), and quickly frozen. Just hook the broad end of the strip (¾ of an inch wide) about ½ inch down from the top of the fillet and drop the combination to the bottom. To properly fish, retrieve the lure in a vertical direction to the surface.

A lake trout will often follow a lure off the bottom and strike from beneath somewhere along its path to the surface. On occasion, you will actually see the trout following the lure. Should this happen, there is little you can do. However, you can try slowing the lure down or stopping its retrieve altogether. Then, jig it around some, while trying to induce a strike.

This technique works best when there's little drift or current. Once the recorder indicates fish, drop the baited lure to the bottom and begin cranking. If the lakers are in a biting mood, they should do the rest.

BAITFISHING

If trolling and jigging aren't your cup of tea, then perhaps you have been waiting for something about baitfishing. Yes, trout and salmon can be caught on bait while surf fishing off the beach and fishing off bulkheads or piers. Here, we will cover baitfishing from shore. Baitfishing from a boat will be discussed in Ch. 14.

Baitfishing from the beach or piers for trout and salmon is admittedly best during the early spring. But during the late spring period we are discussing here, fishing from shore early in the morning often produces. The key thing is temperature. Once water along the shoreline rises above 62 degrees, for all practical purposes baitfishing must be done from a boat. But before that temperature is reached, baits associated with trout can be used while fishing from shore. Salmon and trout eggs make excellent baits. Worms and dead smelt or herring are often fished right on the bottom (but look out for bullheads), and live bait can be suspended under a float and drifted out to the marauding gamefish.

Long, light rods are used while surf casting. Best surf fishing areas include inlets where you can fish off piers into either the inlet itself or the lake. Using from several split-shot up to two ounce sinkers, anglers cast their bait in the general direction of the inlet opening. For live bait suspended under a bobber, simply cast and allow the current to take the bobber in any direction.

For dead baitfish, use a bait holder hook of a size commensurate with the bait you are using. Run the hook through its mouth and out a gill. Fix the hook in its body and pull tight so that the barb is positioned about an inch above the bait's tail.

For spawn bags, simply hide the hook inside a dime sized bag. Fresh spawn works best, but preserved eggs are also used (we will discuss preserving your own eggs in Ch. 19). The bait should be on the end of a 20-inch leader. If worms are being used, you can use the same exact rig. Then, cast out, prop your rod up, and wait! While waiting for a strike, have another rod to cast metal lures like Little Cleos, Phoebes, or Hopkin's metal lures. Early in the morning, before sunrise, is the prime time.

Don't be surprised if you catch some yellow perch while baitfishing in the inlet. Some of the largest perch are caught along the shoreline during this early season, especially on worms. Some of these fish approach 2 pounds and have large humped backs. Perch are also suckers for live bait fished under a bobber.

While fishing with live shiners or herring, run the hook once under the anterior dorsal fin and try keeping the barb of the hook pointed forward. Place the hook about 3½ to 4 feet under a bobber. Cast the combination out as far as you can without damaging the baitfish. Expect the live bait to swim around for some time. Allow them to drift along in the current until they come back in close to shore. Then, reel in, check for liveliness, replace less active ones if necessary, and cast the fresh bait back up current to make the drift again.

FISHING FOR MUSKIES, PIKE AND WALLEYES

*"There are documented cases
of 50-pound muskies chasing
anglers out of a boat. Those
steaknife teeth will rip your hand
to shreds if you let them."*

▼
'9

Soon after the surface temperature of Lake Ontario has risen above 65 degrees, a two-story fishery develops. In the deeper one you can troll (often in the thermocline) for trout and salmon, while in the warmer one you can cast in every little nook and cranny along the shoreline for bass, northern pike, pickerel, perch, panfish, walleye, and muskellunge.

Found everywhere along the shoreline, panfish and perch are very widely dispersed (see Chapter 10). Walleyes can be taken in good numbers from deep river channels which sometimes stretch out into the main lake. Members of the genus Esox — pickerel, northern pike, and muskellunge — provide outstanding action for anyone interested in these fine gamefish.

UP TO 70 POUNDS

Enthusiastic strikers, members of the pike family have been caught in excess of 50 pounds. Although pickerel in Lake Ontario rarely run over 4 pounds, northerns commonly exceed 10 pounds, while the world record musky came in at just under 70!

One of the best and most famous places in the entire world for catching muskies of truly lunker proportions is right here in the northeast corner of Lake Ontario. Called Cape Vincent, the region encompasses the beginning of the St. Lawrence Seaway and the Thousand Islands section of the St. Lawrence River. However, for sheer numbers try the upper Niagara River, a lesser known musky hotspot.

For northern pike, wet a line anywhere along the entire shoreline or in the St. Lawrence River. Found mostly in bays and river mouths emptying into the great lake, northerns feed primarily along weedy shorelines and rarely venture into deep water. True, during the mid part of a summer's day, you may find them down 20 feet or more; but before day's end, they will usually make their way back to feed in shallower water.

Pickerel aren't usually caught in any great numbers, especially where its two cousins are abundant. This may be because the pickerel fry are fed upon heavily by the larger northern fry. Pickerel also remain smaller in size throughout their life cycle and are constantly at risk of being eaten by the larger pike with whom they must share the exact same habitat. Another reason why pickerel aren't that plentiful here is that Lake Ontario is about the northern limit of its range.

However, where eastern chain pickerel are caught on the lake, they strike a multitude of baits and lures, many of them intended for other species (bass, walleye, pike, etc.). Three well regarded places for Ontario pickerel are Little Sodus Bay, Sterling Pond, and Irondequoit Bay. In the summer, pickerel are most active when the lake is very calm, near daybreak. During the day, they can be caught along weedlines, often within several feet of the shore.

Since pickerel look very much like their cousins they are quite often confused with young northern pike and muskies, and anglers catching pickerel often mistakenly report them as such. You should, however, learn the differences, because size and take limits vary among the three species.

Tackle requirements also vary greatly. Muskies being the largest require the heaviest tackle, northerns medium tackle, while pickerel are best enjoyed with light tackle.

MUSKELLUNGE

The Lake Ontario musky season runs from the 3rd Saturday in June until November 30th. The best fishing months are September through October. To be legal, a Lake Ontario musky must be at least 44 inches long except for the upper Niagara River, where a legal fish is 30 inches long. The daily bag limit is one fish per angler. These regulations are subject to change, so always ask for a New York State Regulations Guide whenever you buy your license.

Muskies are not caught all along the Lake Ontario shoreline. As mentioned earlier, you would be wise to concentrate your efforts in the northeast corner of the lake or in the upper Niagara River (above Niagara Falls) between Lake Erie and Lake Ontario. Good locations along the upper Niagara include: Sunken Island, Strawberry Island, Navy Island and Staley's Reef. Note of caution: Unless you are Evil Knievel and wish to shoot Niagara Falls, you'd best not operate your boat north of Grand Island. The restricted zone where boating is strictly forbidden is clearly marked by large signs on both shores.

In the upper northeast corner of Lake Ontario, muskies can be caught at: Wellesley Island; Grindstone Island; Featherbed Shoals; Carleton Island; and Wolfe Island (all of these are in the St. Lawrence); Grenadier Island; Fox Island; Sackets Harbor; and Henderson Harbor. All these locales are within easy reach of Cape Vincent.

Muskies have received quite a reputation over the years as being uncooperative. Fishermen stress persistence as the single most important requirement for success. Some anglers say that it takes about 75 hours of fishing before a keeper sized musky will strike. Well, musky hunters will be glad to know that the average is only 22 hours in the Cape Vincent region. However, that doesn't imply that the fish will be either hooked or landed. With the more favorable odds things can sometimes go right, though, and the Ontario musky angler might catch three or more of these "water tigers" during a single trip.

SPECIFIC MUSKY STRATEGIES

If the main rule for successful musky fishing is persistence, then the second rule must be technique. Angler's logs indicate that most muskies are caught between the hours of 10 AM and 2 PM. It may pay, then, to concentrate on these hours as you try the following techniques.

First, drift into position along musky-holding structure. This might be a fallen log, a rocky bottom, or a weedy shoreline, but it should be in or very close to 6-15 feet of water. Using large lures, begin

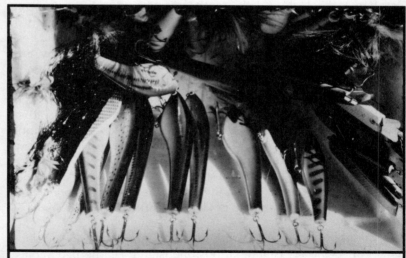

Musky lures are big, tough and sharp — like the fish they're intended for.

casting, making long and accurate casts. Retrieve the lure back to the boat, and continue to drift and cast until your arm is about ready to fall off. Then cast some more! Here's where persistence comes into play. Try to keep all noise coming from the boat to an absolute minimum.

The best results are attained when retrieving lures several feet beneath the surface. You will be surprised when a huge fish flashes up and strikes your lure. Muskies like to follow and strike from under the lure, and more times than not, a rewarding trip may be nothing more than seeing a huge, fearsome hulk trailing along beneath your lure.

Should a musky follow your lure, great! Make note of its presence. Although sticking your rod tip into the water and zipping your lure around in a figure eight pattern while attempting to draw a strike is often quoted as a good technique, you would do much better to simply change your lure and continue casting. But, no matter what, the territorial musky will not venture too far from where it has been seen. Mark the location and make certain to fish in the very same area again later in the day or even sometime the next day or later in the week.

"Let's work that rock ledge over there," Mike said, "and see if we can't get that musky that swiped our smallmouth bass yesterday. He had to go close to 40 inches long, don't you think?"

We shut off the engine on our 14-foot boat and lazily slid in towards the low cliffs that dropped into the water along the shoreline. This was just south of Sackets Harbor, in an area named for an old abandoned "oil rig."

"Fine with me," I replied as I reached for my musky rod and made certain that my Mepp's Muskie Killer was firmly attached to the short wire leader on the end of my line.

"What are you using?" I asked my partner, outdoor writer, Mike Kersey.

"I'm going with this yellow Swim Whizz."

Soon we were within range of the shoreline just about where the big fish had taken our smallmouth bass for lunch the day before.

Ten casts, twenty casts . . . fifty casts or more went by without the slightest response. Then all of a sudden, like a streak of lightning crashing into the water, a huge musky flashed up and creamed Mike's Swim Whizz.

"Holy cow!" Mike exclaimed as the monster made for places unknown.

Within 10 minutes of the strike, the just legal size musky was on its side making ever smaller circles in the water as he approached us. Carefully, I reached over the rail and attempted to lift the beautifully colored fish into the boat.

Surprisingly enough, the big fish was ready and offered no resistance.

"Not bad for a beginner," I teased Mike as I snapped off a few pictures before easing the large musky over the gunwale and back into the cold water. "Now, let's get his daddy."

Musky fishermen have quite an assortment of lures at their disposal. From swimming plugs (like the one Mike was using) to giant spinners, most musky tempters are large replicas of popular bass lures. For starters, stick to several lures and learn how to work them well. One of the best known is a spinner called the Mepp's Muskie Killer. Fished in either all black or yellow colors, it may account for more "Esox" strikes than any other lure. Some other favorites include Bagley's Deep Diving Bang-O-Lure; Swim Whizz straight and jointed; Creek Chub Jointed Pike; Suick; "B" Flat Shiner and Teddy surface action jerk baits; Jointed Smity crankbaits; giant double

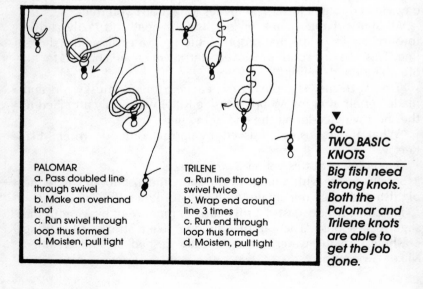

PALOMAR
a. Pass doubled line through swivel
b. Make an overhand knot
c. Run swivel through loop thus formed
d. Moisten, pull tight

TRILENE
a. Run line through swivel twice
b. Wrap end around line 3 times
c. Run end through loop thus formed
d. Moisten, pull tight

▼
9a.
TWO BASIC KNOTS

Big fish need strong knots. Both the Palomar and Trilene knots are able to get the job done.

tandem spinnerbaits; and my favorite the extra large buzzbaits. Of course, giant spoons and the jig and pig combination (bucktail jig and a piece of pork rind) can't be forgotten.

If you simply get too tired to cast anymore, and that can happen, you can also fish live bait for muskellunge. Since a musky will attack and eat just about anything foolish enough to swim through its lair, the choice is large. You can use large suckers, lamprey eels, river chubs, or extra large golden shiners. Rig the bait with a trailing treble hook protruding off a wire harness. Then, swim the bait livelined or under a float into areas where muskies are known to roam.

When a musky takes the bait, give him just enough time to swallow it. Once he has, the wire harness will protect your line from the fish's razor sharp teeth. Wait about 10 seconds and then slam the set of treble hooks home. With that, your hooks should be solidly embedded into the fish's jaw. Remember, muskies like to strike from the bottom up, so keep your bait well off the bottom.

One last but not least technique is trolling. This can be effective when an appropriate lure is trolled slowly through musky habitat. Make certain, first of all, to concentrate on water that is under 15 feet deep. Although muskies may hold deeper, they rarely if ever feed deeper! Then look for a rocky bottom, where cliffs fall into the water, at the ends of islands, along weedy shorelines, and where trees or other fixed debris has fallen into the lake or river. Spoons and crankbaits make the best lures to troll. Also, make certain to net (not gaff) your prize, since gaffing muskies is against the law on Lake Ontario.

There are documented cases of 50-pound muskies chasing anglers out of a boat. Be careful — those steaknife teeth will rip your hand to shreds if you let them.

NORTHERN PIKE AND PICKEREL

While muskellunge is accurately called "the fish of a thousand casts," northern pike and pickerel tend to be pleasantly more co-operative. With a long fishing season lasting from the 1st Saturday in May through the following March 15th, you can fish for them almost year round. In truth, there really aren't enough pickerel that many fish for them exclusively. But the pickerel will often be found side by side with pike and can be thus discussed concurrently with the much more highly sought northern.

These fish feed heavily early in the morning along weed beds. Then, as the day progresses, they rest while digesting their food. Later on towards afternoon, they become hungry again and remain quite active on into darkness.

Good locations to catch northern pike include: in the lower Niagara River between Fort Niagara and Youngstown in the spring when they move in to spawn; in Twelve Mile Creek by Wilson's Harbor; in Hopkin's Creek located west of Olcott Harbor; in Eighteen Mile Creek at Olcott; in Johnson's Creek; in Oak Orchard Creek; in Braddocks Bay and Salmon Creek; in Irondequoit Bay and occasionally in the Creek; in Sodus Bay; Port Bay; Little Sodus Bay; in the Salmon River; in North and South "Sandy" Pond; in the Lakeview Wildlife Management Area by the South Sandy and Sandy Creeks; in Henderson Harbor; in Sackets Harbor; in Chaumont Bay; off Point Peninsula, Fox and Grenadier Islands; and from the mouth of the St. Lawrence Seaway everywhere to Wellesley Island.

TACKLE TO DO THE JOB

Medium action 6-7 foot baitcasting and spinning outfits are all that's required for northerns; because of their lesser size, pickerel should be fished for with ultra-light tackle. However, if you want, you can fish for both species using the same tackle. A good compromise outfit would be a light to medium action 6-foot baitcasting or spinning rod with matching reel loaded with from 6-10 pound test line.

While bait fishing for northern pike and pickerel, stick to spinning outfits and large minnows. Although these gamefish can be caught on worms, frogs, crabs, or almost anything that moves, minnows make up over 90% of their diet. When casting bait, use a 9-12 inch thin wire leader between your line and a size #4-6 baitholder hook. Keep the bait about three feet below a float. Sometimes a split-shot is required on the line between the bait and bobber. After casting, it is wise to use a Strike Guard or, at least, keep your bail open. This should preclude any possibility of a big fish grabbing your bait and pulling your rod into the water (it can happen!).

Once a northern pike or pickerel takes the bait, your bobber will "blurp" as it disappears under the water and quickly heads for the

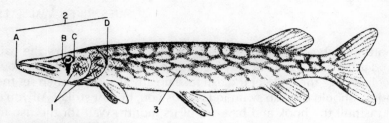

CHAIN PICKEREL *(Esox niger)*

1. Cheeks And Gill Cover Fully Scaled.
2. Distance From Tip Of Snout (a) To Front Of Eye (b) Greater Than Distance From Back Of Eye (c) To End Of Gill Cover (d).
3. Chain-Like Pattern On Sides Of Adults.

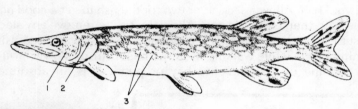

NORTHERN PIKE *(Esox lucius)*

1. Cheek Fully Scaled.
2. Opercle Scaled Only On Upper Half.
3. Yellow Bean-Like Spots On Sides

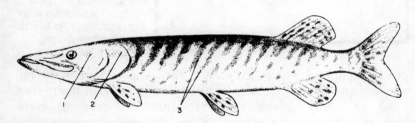

MUSKELLUNGE *(Esox masquinongy)*

1. Cheek Scaled Only On Upper Half.
2. Opercle Scaled Only On Upper Half.
3. Side Plain Or With Vertical Bars.

▶ *9b. IDENTIFYING PICKEREL, PIKE AND MUSKELLUNGE*

bottom. After a short period of time, the fish will swallow the bait and attempt to swim away. When you observe line coming off your reel, engage the bail, let the fish take up any slack, and then set the hook. Should the fish swim in towards you, do not strike! All you'll do is pull the hook and bait out of its mouth. Wait for the fish to turn around and start swimming away. Have patience. Then, when he does make his move, set the hook.

Another good bait fishing technique is to use a long shanked hook and a dead minnow. Hook the minnow up through both its lips and cast, without weight, as far as possible. Then, retrieve while twitching the rod tip to impart action into the lifeless bait. Do this all the way back to you. When a pike or pickerel strikes, open your bail. Allow a second or two for the fish to get a good hold on the bait, then close the bail. Allow the fish to remove any slack, and set the hook as before. This technique is best employed using spinning tackle while walking or if in a boat drifting slowly around the shoreline of your favorite bay or pond. It is an absolutely

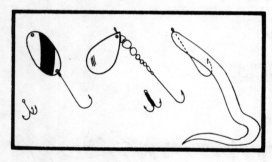

▼
9c.
ADAPTING LURES FOR PICKEREL AND PIKE
Try removing the trebles and replacing with a long shanked hook, which you can rig to be weedless with the addition of a Texas style rubber worm.

deadly technique when used early in the season or late in the fall.

There are a multitude of pike and pickerel lures on the market. Most are similar to bass lures and include surface plugs, crankbaits, deep divers, jigs and pigs, spoons, spinners, spinnerbaits, and buzzbaits.

An excellent lure may be made by modifying a buzzbait. Take the rubber skirt off the buzzbait and add a Mann's Auger Frog or Auger Grubtail in its place. The lure is extremely effective and virtually weedless.

Another adaptation may be made to a spinning lure. Remove its treble hook and replace with a single, long-shanked hook. Make it weedless by adding a Mr. Twister tail or a rubber worm (Texas Style) to the hook (see Fig. 9-c). The long hook and worm will make a good target for the pike or pickerel to strike. This will also keep them well away from your line, making it less likely that they will be able to bite through it.

For maximum success, fish these adaptations in and around lily pads and weed beds. After the lure hits the water, make as much commotion as possible before slowly reeling it back. If the pike or pickerel are cooperating, you just may see one jump out of the water and come down on top of the lure. There's little in the world of angling as exciting as this!

Northern pike can also be trolled. Two distinct schools of thought have evolved about trolling for northerns. School one has you troll slowly along all the usual haunts, while the other school calls for speeding up. Called "speed trolling," this latter technique requires that the lure vibrate intensely as it comes through the water. This intense action triggers ferocious strikes so if you fish this way, you best be using musky tackle. When a northern pike strikes a fast moving lure, any line under 15 pound test is liable to break.

WALLEYED PIKE

Tops as tablefare, walleye is a much pursued species. Although not too powerful, they grow large and can be caught on very light tackle at many different northern tier and a few southern tier locations. Caught primarily in river mouths, good populations exist in the Black River between Bull Rock Point and the Dexter Channel; in North "Sandy" Pond by tributary bridges early in the spring; in the Oswego River Channel and by the dam both spring and fall; in the middle of Sodus Bay; in the Genesee River; in Golden Hill Creek; and in the Niagara River. Walleyes grow to good sizes in this lake and 6 pounders are not uncommon. Not too many people fish specifically for walleye in Lake Ontario, but if you want to work for them, you can score.

The walleye season in Lake Ontario runs from the 1st Saturday in May until March 15th. Your daily bag limit is three fish 18 inches or larger. At the start of the season, the best walleye technique is to troll a weight forward spinner, like a Mepp's Lusox, in combination with a nightcrawler through the often tightly grouped schools of fish. Look for them to be suspended off the bottom in from 20-40 feet of water. Continue trolling through the schools, or drift and cast the weight forward spinners into the fish and expect outstanding action. Other weight forward spinners include: Erie Dearies; Hildebrant's Gold and Silver Nuggets; West Sister Twisters; and Parrish Lures.

Often walleyes are caught by anglers in pursuit of other species. Bass fishermen commonly catch walleyes while casting lures towards banks of weeds. Walleyes are extremely light sensitive and will hide from the sun. Therefore, good bass structure which offers much shade also attracts Mr. Marble Eye!

There are good types of trolling lures, and one is the crankbait. Some of the better producers are the Wiggle Wart, Hot N' Tot, Shad Rap, and Countdown Rapala. Spoons also catch walleyes and interested downrigger fishermen can try the Northport Nailer and Flutter Chuck. Best temperatures for walleyes are 60-70 degrees. Best times include very early in the morning and then again at dusk on into darkness.

As the season progresses walleyes return to the bottom and can be caught using a jig and minnow combination. Cast and retrieve until a strike is encountered. Once you catch the first walleye, mark the spot. They are schooling fish and more strikes will be sure to follow. Some hot walleye jigs are the Tinsel Tail, Ugly Bug, Fuzz-E-Grub, and Mr. Twister. Fished alone or in combination with minnows, leeches, or nightcrawlers, these lures are proven walleye takers.

One of the best times of year to catch walleyes is during late autumn when the air is getting cold. If there's a heavy frost on the ground and your finger tips are numb, the time is right!

FISHING FOR BASS AND PANFISH

"Once hooked, smallmouth never seem to quit. They make leap after leap often coming down with loud resounding "whoops." These fish are truly exciting!"

10

Largemouth and smallmouth bass, two of America's most prized freshwater fish, are caught in good numbers and sizes in Lake Ontario. In addition, there are panfish by the millions, including crappie (both white and black), freshwater drum, rock bass, white bass, perch (both white and yellow), sunfish and bluegills, catfish, smelt and carp. You can catch bass and panfish in bays, harbors, rivers and along the shoreline off piers, jetties, and beaches. Panfish are available year round, while the bass can only be taken in season. The best thing about these species is that they are very cooperative and a good catch is assured almost anytime.

LARGEMOUTH BASS
Found in all coves, river mouths, ponds, and other backwaters spread along the periphery of Lake Ontario, these fish grow quite large with lunkers weighing in the neighborhood of five pounds. The bass in Lake Ontario spawn generally between mid-May and mid-June, and to help them do so, the fishing season remains closed until the 3rd Saturday in June. In season, you are allowed to keep five bass in aggregate in excess of 12 inches in the big lake. There are certain exceptions in tributary rivers, for example bass need only be 10 inches if caught above the Peace Bridge in the upper Niagara River. The bass fishing season closes on November 30th.

Late in the spring, the backwaters warm up quickly. Water temperatures rise into the mid to upper 70's, even though out in the main lake temperatures remain consistently lower. This causes largemouth, which prefer the low seventies, to remain in these locations, while smallmouth, which prefer the high sixties, vacate the bays and enter the main lake.

After this separation early in June, smallmouth bass become readily accessible to anglers fishing off piers, from the surf, and out in boats. This is because they mingle and feed right along the shoreline. However the largemouth bass actually becomes less accessible. Because of limited backwater accessibility (many marshy, swampy areas, or private sections) largemouth are best fished from a boat at this time. Because of this situation, smallmouth are much more popular in this region.

WHERE TO FISH FOR BUCKETMOUTHS
Following are some of the better largemouth bass locations along

Lake Ontario. Because there are so many good spots, we have put them in list form:

The lower Niagara River (although not too abundant here)
Four Mile Creek
The West and East Branches of 12 Mile Creek at Wilson
18 Mile Creek near Olcott
Johnson Creek near Lakeside Park
Oak Orchard Creek near Point Breeze
Sandy Creek near North Hamlin
Braddocks Bay
Cranberry Pond
Long Pond
Buck Pond
The Genesee River
Irondequoit Bay
Sodus Bay
Port Bay
Little Sodus Bay
Blind Sodus Bay
The Pond at Fair Haven
The Oswego River
The Little Salmon River estuary
The Salmon River estuary
Sandy Pond (both North and South ponds)
Henderson Harbor
Sackets Harbor
The Thousand Islands section of the St. Lawrence River

Most of these locations offer boat launches, tackle shops, and local guide services, and many have boat liveries where you can rent a small boat and motor for a day.

One of the best lures used on Lake Ontario's bucketmouths is the rubber worm. Dark colors, such as purple, black, and motor oil work best. Worms 6-10 inches long rigged "Texas Style" look like young lamprey eels and catch largemouth bass in good numbers. A Texas Rig, one of many ways of rigging a rubber worm, is virtually weedless. The eye of the hook is buried in the worm, and sometimes held in place with a segment of toothpick. The point and barb of

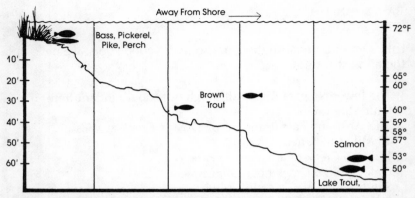

Away From Shore ⟶

72°F

Bass, Pickerel,
Pike, Perch

10'
20' — 65°
— 60°
30'
Brown
Trout
40' — 60°
— 59°
50' — 58°
— 57°
60' Salmon
— 53°
— 50°
Lake Trout,

▶ *10a. JUNE FISHERY— Once the lake stratifies, bass, pike, and panfish*
remain abundant inshore, but coldwater species move offshore and
seek water temperatures that may be quite deep.

the hook are brought around and placed back into the worm.
Often, a torpedo weight is added directly ahead of the worm, but
sometimes the worm is fished without weight.

Cast this rigged worm at docks, into fallen timber, or directly into
fields of lily pads, such as those found in the Little Salmon River. As
the worm settles, watch your line carefully. Often, bass will scoop
it up and swim away. When this happens, point the tip of your rod
at the fleeting line. Allow the fish to take up any slack, then pull
back on your rod and set the hook.

Should the bass pick up the worm and swim in toward you,
quickly reel in the slack line and strike as he's about to either swim
by or under your position. Should nothing strike the worm, reel up
any slack line and raise the tip of your rod directly over your head
thereby allowing the worm to drop back down to the bottom.
Continue this procedure all the way back to your position.

Other lures, for example surface plugs, are used early in the
morning along weedy shorelines like those found in the back of
Port Bay, Sodus Bay, and North "Sandy" Pond. Select a size #11
floating Rebel or Rapala, or the 3½ inch Bagley Bang-O-lure, a
Bomber Minnow, a Cotton Cordell Red-fin, a Devil Horse, a Zara
Spook, or a Mann's Mann Dancer. All you have to do is cast and
retrieve. If a bass wants the lure, he'll crash the surface and take it.

Besides rubber worms and surface plugs, you should collect a
wide variety of spinnerbaits. Used in deeper water (largemouths

are rarely found in water over 15 feet deep), these lures imitate baitfish and take bass along weedlines found in such locations as North "Sandy" Pond, Henderson Harbor, the Niagara River, the Salmon River, and Irondequoit Bay.

FLY RODDING POSSIBLE

For fly rodders, poppers and streamers are effective. There's plenty of room to cast along the shores of the bays so use an 8-foot fly rod with DT floating line and a 7-foot leader with tip strength from 4-6 pounds. Cast a streamer or popper directly into marshy areas such as those by Long and Buck Ponds; near Wolcott Creek in Port Bay; along the reeds behind The Pond in Fair Haven State Park; in the

Salmon River estuary; in South "Sandy" Pond; and in Lakeview Marsh by Sandy Creek. After casting, allow the fly or popper to rest for a moment and then slowly jerk it back.

For crankbaits, try the Big Bad Leroy Brown, the Sonic (especially in off-colored water, as in the Genesee River or after a storm elsewhere), the Big "O" and Deep "O" series, the Rat-L-Trap, the Thin Fin, the Hot N' Tot, the Crawdad, the Fin Mann, or other types of yellow, green, and orange crankbaits.

Spinning lures and spoons can also be used effectively. Fished slowly or trolled, bass are often fooled into striking these minnow imitators. They are best fished near drop-offs such as you'll find by

Outdoor writer Dave Mann with a fine largemouth from North "Sandy" Pond. Ontario's bucketmouth population is quite good in some of these warmer backwaters.

Helds Cove in Irondequoit Bay, along the Niagara River, and along the rocky shoreline surrounding the Nine Mile Atomic Power Plant in Mexico Bay.

Another acceptable method used to catch bass on Lake Ontario is with live bait. Minnows, golden shiners, herring, frogs, leeches, or nightcrawlers all take bass. Use size #4-6 baitholder hooks, add weight only if necessary (to cast or hold bottom), and fish as light as possible. Lines should range between 4-6 pound test. Spinning rods are best adapted to such light lines and live baits.

Use minnows and golden shiners generally in the 3-4 inch range. Run a hook under the dorsal fin of the baitfish, add a bobber above and cast the bait gently to keep it alive. Large Golden Shiners (5-7 inches) make excellent trophy bait, and while you may go an entire season without a strike, if you get one stand by!

Trophy bass fishing is done with fairly heavy tackle and often with live bait. Using a big float and a baitcasting outfit with no less than 10 pound test line, run a large #4 baitholder hook underneath the shiner's anal fin and hold it above some large lily pads in a big lily-pad field. Then drop the shiner in, nose first, so he can swim under the pads. Allow him to work there for hours if necessary.

Herring baits should be fished under bobbers or live-lined. These baits are very fragile and will die quickly if not handled properly. To keep herring alive as long as possible use a round bait bucket, O-Tabs or electric aerator for oxygen, and ice to keep the water cool. Hook the herring carefully under the dorsal fin and allow it to swim freely away from the boat. If the herring stays up too high in the water, add a split-shot.

With frogs, run the hook up through both lips and cast to the shoreline. Allow the frog to swim in any direction. Expect a strike when fishing early in the morning, late in the afternoon, or after dark. Big bass love frogs, and many lunkers are caught by this method annually in Lake Ontario.

Nightcrawlers are commonly used and effective on bass. Simply string the big worm on a #4-6 baitholder hook (or three hook harness), add some weight, and cast. Either allow the bait to stay in one location, or bring the bait slowly along the bottom. Bass and panfish will intercept somewhere along the line. A simple way to make a three hook harness is to buy a rubber worm already rigged that way. Carefully remove the rubber worm from the harness and add the real thing.

At nighttime, largemouth bass will feed along the shoreline. This means that they will vacate the areas where they have been lurking during the day and move in close to the beach. There, they will feed actively upon frogs, minnows, crayfish (crabs), salamanders, leeches, and their all time favorite food, the golden shiner!

Best nighttime action is from right after darkness falls until about midnight. Then, after a slack period, the action often increases around 4 AM and lasts until dawn. So, either consider fishing until midnight, or begin around 4 AM. Fishing is best on dark, moonless nights.

SMALLMOUTH BASS

More popular in this region than the largemouth bass, and considered by many to be "pound for pound" the hardest fighting freshwater fish, smallmouth bass are extremely abundant in Lake Ontario. Found around the entire periphery of the lake, smallmouth prefer colder water temperatures than the largemouth (optimum for smallmouth is 65-69 degrees and largemouth 70-75 degrees). Therefore, the smallmouth often take up residence outside the warmer areas where the largemouths are found. Temperatures in the region greatly favor the smallmouth to the largemouth, and many more smallies reach lunker proportions in excess of 4 pounds (a largemouth, to be considered a lunker, would have to be over 6 pounds and that's not too common on Lake Ontario). Smallmouth also tend to school more than the largemouth and if you catch one smallmouth, chances are good that you will catch more.

There are probably few places in the world where the smallmouth fishing is better. When the bass season opens (3rd Saturday in June), the overall water temperature in the bays and rivers is usually around 60 degrees (surface is much warmer). At this temperature, the smallmouth bass become very active. They chase lures and bite well on all kinds of live baits. Once hooked, smallmouth never seem to quit. They make leap after leap often coming down with loud resounding "whoops" as they hit the water. These fish are truly exciting!

After a short period of time, the rapid warming of the inland backwaters chases most smallmouth out into the cooler waters found around the shoreline of the main lake. So, let's look now at these waters and see where you stand the best chance to catch a mess of these good fighting fish.

WHERE TO CATCH BRONZEBACKS

Since all smallmouth bass love rocky bottoms, you must primarily look for and find good rock cover. To best help you locate these bassy positions, you may want to invest in the Great Lakes Map Series, 14803, 14804, 14805, and 14806 published by the U.S. Department of Commerce. In this series of navigation maps, rocky bottoms are indicated with the symbol "RKY."

As we locate these prime smallmouth bass areas for you, mark them down on your maps. Lacking the navigation maps, even a road map will do. We will mention both common and local area names, but it will be up to you to pin-point each location. We could also give you the Loran coordinates of these locations, but if you need these coordinates, they may be found on the government maps mentioned above.

We will begin in the southwest corner of the lake at the Niagara River and work our way east along the bottom of the lake and up the eastern shoreline to Cape Vincent or the beginning of the Thousand Islands.

In the Niagara River, fish Devils Hole Drift, just upstream of the *Hydro-Electric Power Commission of Ontario's* power plant and the Robert Moses Power Project. Expect good to excellent smallmouth productivity in this stretch. Below here, on the Canadian side, Bullhead Bay is a good bet along with Peggy's Eddy further along on the U.S. side. The Fort George Drift across from Fort Niagara State Park and the Coast Guard Drift directly in front of the State Park offer excellent smallmouth bass fishing for trollers and drifters alike.

Moving east along the southern shoreline, you can catch smallmouth bass at Twelve Mile Creek. Largemouths and northerns are caught along with the smallies in this creek, which is hot in the late spring when the bass season opens. Smallmouth move out of the creek in the summer, but then return again later in the fall. In the harbor at Wilson formed by both the east and west branches of the creek, all species can be caught.

At Olcott, another quaint fishing village on Ontario's southern shore, smallmouth and largemouth bass, northern pike, and panfish can all be caught in the harbor, along the inlet pier, and throughout the expanse of the creek up to Burt Dam. There are all sorts of fishing shops and eateries catering to fishermen in the area.

Moving east, you come to Golden Hill Creek and Marsh Creek

where smallmouth can be taken, but the big attraction here is offshore and west of Johnson Creek where the bottom is 16 feet down and very rocky. You can also reach this area by exiting Green Harbor and traveling east.

Following in rapid succession come more rocky bottom areas called: Orchard Point Shoal, Hamlin Beach State Park, and Wautoma Shoal (which is east of Sandy Creek Harbor). Braddocks Bay Channel also has a rocky bottom and is considered a smallmouth hotspot. Excellent fishing exists for those using live bait, jigging, and trolling in these areas.

Often overlooked, the Genesee River has quite a sizable small-mouth population. Bass are caught both above and below the falls at Driving Park Road, but only those caught below the falls can venture forth into the big lake. If you have never seen the Genesee River, it is quite unique. It runs directly through the City of Rochester; however, it is way down in a steep canyon. Only where the Genesee empties into the lake is it readily accessible other than by boat.

Just east of the Genesee River is Irondequoit Bay. In this big expanse of water smallmouth bass show up on occasion in the inlet where there are two new fishing jetties. East of Irondequoit Bay is Webster Park. The park features a fishing pier and plenty of parking, but further to the east and offshore lies Nine Mile Point where there's a good rocky bottom and plenty of smallmouth. Still further east, you pass the R.E. Ginna Atomic Power Plant and the Pultney-ville Harbor where more good bottom is found.

Maxwell Creek is just west of Sodus Point. There is good fishing here when the creek itself is running strong. This is usually the case early in the spring when smallmouth can be taken just offshore on brown jigs. At Sodus, bass can be caught all along the breakfront and pier that extend well out into Lake Ontario on both the eastern and western shores. Although the floating variety of lures catch smallmouth, sinking Rebels, Rapalas, and Baglies are much more effective. Cast them out and let them sink for a few counts before retrieving them back to you. Big smallmouth may intercept anywhere along the way in this area. Best fishing is offered on threatening and rainy days when there is reduced boat traffic.

Port Bay also harbors a good smallmouth population all season long. It has an excellent public boat launch ramp (plus there's another at Pier One). From these locations, you can be outside the inlet in minutes. Fish in from 10-30 feet of water. There's good rocky

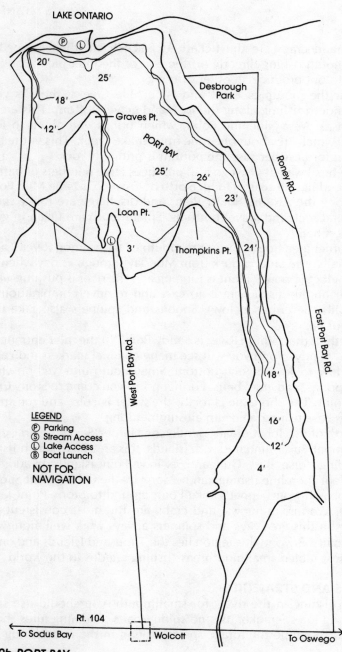

LAKE ONTARIO

Ⓟ Ⓛ

20'

25'

Desbrough
Park

18'

Graves Pt.

12'

PORT BAY

Roney Rd.

25'

26'

Loon Pt.

23'

Ⓛ

3'

21'

Thompkins Pt.

West Port Bay Rd.

East Port Bay Rd.

18'

16'

LEGEND
Ⓟ Parking
Ⓢ Stream Access
Ⓛ Lake Access
Ⓑ Boat Launch

12'

**NOT FOR
NAVIGATION**

4'

Rt. 104

To Sodus Bay

Wolcott

To Oswego

▶ *10b. PORT BAY*

cover, and crabs are the ticket! At Fair Haven, there's excellent smallmouth fishing directly off the end of the inlet piers. Look for crabs to out produce all other offerings.

Near the mouth of Eight and Nine Mile Creeks, there is good smallmouth fishing along the rock and gravel bottom. This area is known as West Ninemile Point, which brings you along to Ford Shoals which are about one mile from Snake Creek. This entire area is good for bass because the bottom is primarily rock.

The breakwall at Oswego also produces large numbers of bass on crabs and jigs all season long. North of Oswego is Nine Mile Point. All along the Atomic Power Plant and discharge are rocky shorelines and rock and gravel bottoms. Smallmouth are taken in good numbers here!

Another area hotspot is in the mouth of the Salmon River. This is especially true around dusk from Monday through Friday when the hydro-electric power plant is running and the river is pushing water. The technique used here is to cast and retrieve combinations of bucktails (described below). Spoons and spinners also take their share of bass.

North of the Salmon River is Sandy Pond. In the inlet entrance to North "Sandy" Pond you will see many channel markers indicating a shallow, rocky, irregular bottom. Smallmouth bite well on crabs, jigs, spoons, and crankbaits. Further north you come to Stony Creek and Point. The shoreline is rocky, the water is cold, and the smallmouth bass fishing holds up all summer long.

North of this location are Henderson Harbor, Sackets Harbor, and Chaumont Bay. Inundated with islands, this area has many hotspots including Horse, Bass, Gull, and Six Town Point Islands. In addition, excellent shoreline fishing can be done by the Oil Rig near Sackets Harbor, and from Tippet's Lake Point around to Stony Point Lighthouse. Worms, minnows, and crabs are the most consistent producers in this area. Jigs and spinners always work well along with crankbaits. Beyond this region lies the Thousand Islands and one of the most fabled smallmouth bass fishing regions in the world.

LURES AND STRATEGIES

When fishing in the rivers for smallmouth, you should use small spinning lures, crankbaits, and spinnerbaits. Spinning lures should closely resemble the forage species found in the river during that

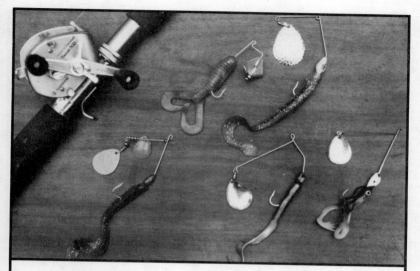

Try replacing the skirts on your favorite spinnerbaits and buzz-baits with an augur grub tail or worm. Bass and pike love 'em this way!

particular time. Since small herring are usually present, use Mepp's silver spinners, Fox spinners, and CP Swings.

For spinnerbaits, use small frames with white and light blue skirts. These combinations closely resemble herring. Still in the crankbait category, Storm Lure's ThinFin silver shad is a good choice. Not only does it look like a herring, but when retrieved in a slow and steady motion, it also swims like one.

Fish these lures in deep river riffles, and alongside fallen timber. Smallmouth like swift currents. They will usually strike when your lure swings around beneath you in the current. Big fish tend not to chase lures. For them, fish very near the bottom. In still water, retrieve lures slowly along the surface stopping every now and then.

Once the smallmouth move out of the rivers and take up residence along these rocky bottom sections of shoreline, they remain and feed all day. But as evening approaches, they form schools or "wolf packs" and venture out from these daytime havens in search of other food. Their travels take them in toward the beach or into inlets where they feed heavily upon herring. When fishing along

the beach or near inlets early in the evening, look for diving birds to give away their presence.

When bass are feeding near river mouths, like those of the Salmon and Niagara Rivers, another excellent lure choice is a bucktail jig combination. Tie a heavy jig, such as Mann's Little George bucktail on your line and make a dropper loop about 18 inches above. Then, add a small maribou bucktail to the loop. The best maribou bucktails weigh between 1/32 and 1/64 ounce while the preferred color for these jigs is either all yellow, black, brown or white.

Trolling on the big lake and in navigable rivers is very productive on smallmouth bass. Mepp's #1 flutter spoons, Little Cleos, Phoebes, and streamer flies are all good choices, but Lake Ontario's favorite is the crankbait. For best results, crankbaits should imitate either small baitfish or crayfish.

Although you can take smallmouth bass quite effectively on lures, most Lake Ontario anglers prefer to fish for them using live bait. The most often used live bait in this region is the crayfish or in the local vernacular "crabs." However, the most effective crab is one that has a soft shell. Nightcrawlers make an excellent second choice and you can certainly catch smallmouth on minnows, too.

You can fish crabs off a pier or from an anchored or drifting boat. If fishing off a pier or an anchored boat, cast out and slowly retrieve the offering along the bottom. If drifting, follow these instructions passed along by noted Lake Ontario bass fisherman and guide Capt. Charlie De Noto, (owner of Pier One in Port Bay). Run a heavy weight (twenty pounds or more) down a strong line to the bottom. Use this weight to rough up the bottom as it is bounced along by the drifting boat. As this occurs, crayfish and aquatic insects will be dislodged and float away in the current. Smallmouth bass crossing this trail of edible material will follow it back to the boat where, hopefully, they will encounter your bait which must be fished in very close to the dragging weight. Old window sashes, several bricks (the kind with holes in the middle) tied together, or a bucket half full of cement serve very well in this capacity. Another purpose served by the weight is to slow down your drift. Your crabs will creep along more slowly, giving bass a better opportunity to pounce upon them.

ZANE GRAY ON SMALLMOUTH

For those of you truly interested in catching a lunker smallmouth bass, listen to the timeless advice given by the great Zane Gray in his "Tales of Fishing" published in 1928. He stated, while talking about lunker smallmouth bass: They are old and wary. I never caught one in deep water. I never had one take hold nearer than one hundred feet from the boat. I never caught one on the day I first saw him. I never caught a very large bass, say over five pounds, until after the beginning of the harvest moon. Furthermore, I know that these big bass do not feed often.

With these words of admonishment, take heed! Big bass are truly wise critters!

Some terrific panfishing awaits the angler visiting Lake Ontario. All around the lake there are public piers, jetties, boat launches and beaches where fine panfish catches can be made. And with yellow perch, white perch, smelt, sunfish, bullhead, giant rock bass, white bass, crappies, and carp all growing to good sizes (plus exotic species such as the freshwater drum), you should never pass up an opportunity to fish for these cooperative species.

PERCH, PERCH EVERYWHERE

Yellow perch prefer the warm waters of the lake, although they are caught easily in great numbers through the ice. They are a schooling fish that are rather inactive at night. Caught well on small to medium shiners and worms, perch will also strike a wide variety of lures. Found all along the entire shoreline, perch become a valuable gamefish forage when herring and smelt are in short supply. Perch have an excellent taste and are highly regarded as a food fish around the lake.

White perch is one of the best eating fish found anywhere. Whites usually remain quite deep in the lake all day long. But, as late afternoon approaches, they slowly make their way into the shore-line where they feed heavily upon small fish, insects, and other food which they may find there. They're not strong fighters, so light tackle is recommended. White perch may be taken on small bass bugs and many different dry fly patterns, making them a good subject for ultra-light fly fishing.

SUNNIES AND "CATS"
Sunfish are all over the place. For the most fun use two pound test line and tiny sunny poppers. Just cast out and watch the sunfish come up behind and strike the lure. This method can really test your reflexes.

For baitfishing, nothing outfishes the common earthworm. Simply place one or a piece of one on a hook and suspend it beneath a bobber. Fish it wherever there's water and you should encounter the cooperative sunfish.

Brown bullhead are found in good numbers along the southern tier, where they prefer muddy bottoms and slow moving streams. Along with their cousins the black catfish and channel cat, they are caught on worms, crayfish, and minnows, and they are largely night feeders. Catfish make excellent eating. Some specific places to seek them are the East and West Branches of 12 Mile Creek, Johnson Creek, Oak Orchard Creek, Buck Pond, Long Pond, Cranberry Pond, Braddocks Bay, Genesee River, Irondequoit Bay, Pultneyville, Sodus Bay, Port Bay, Little Sodus Bay, and Oswego Bay.

OTHER PANFISH
Rock bass (red eye) grow really large in this lake. Averaging around a pound apiece, they take minnows, worms, grubs, grasshoppers, crickets and flies with alacrity. Considering their size, these fish can put up quite a struggle on the end of light tackle.

They are most fun to catch on spinnerbaits, especially with rubber frogs rather than rubber skirts for primary targets. Spinners and crayfish crankbaits make good choices very early in the morning and again very late in the afternoon. Fish for them at the Niagara River, Wilson Harbor, off piers at Fair Haven, off the

Fresh water drum is one of Ontario's less promoted species. They are, nonetheless, considered to be good tablefare. This fish is also call "Sheepshead."

bulkhead in Oswego Harbor, in the Little Salmon and Salmon Rivers, and in Henderson Harbor.

White bass (silver bass) like deep water sections of swift moving rivers and depressions found in ponds. They feed in tight schools and can sometimes be caught by the bucket load. They feed well on minnows and worms. For lures, try jigs, small crankbaits, and spinners. White bass feed well all day long, but are most active at dusk and into darkness along the shoreline. Look for them at the Coast Guard Drift on the Niagara River.

Crappies, both white and black, are also worthy targets. These fish are big minnow eaters and can be effectively taken on miniature 1/32 oz. all yellow or white marabou bucktails. Fish the small bucktails alone with a fly rod, or behind a bobber with a spinning rod. Cast up to the shoreline and work slowly back to you. Once a crappie is encountered, look out! These are thickly schooling fish and undoubtedly, more crappies will be caught in the very same area once you have located the school. A few hot fishing areas are Wilson Harbor, Port Bay, and Oswego Harbor.

Carp are residents of many backwater areas and can be caught on corn, dough balls, cheese balls, earthworms, crabs, or bread. The best way to bring carp into the area where you are fishing is to chum often with whole kernel corn. Soon, carp will begin to hang around for a free meal. However, after several days of freebies, slip a hook into the corn and have yourself a ball.

Some good locations to catch carp include Braddocks Bay, Buck Pond, Cranberry Pond, Round Pond, Irondequoit Bay, Sodus Bay, and Port Bay. Although summer is considered prime time, you can catch carp wherever the water is ice free.

Freshwater drum (sheepshead) are found in large rivers, harbors, and bays such as the Niagara River and the Oswego Harbor. Although they can be caught in the lake, most fishing takes place off bulkheads while using worms, minnows, and crayfish for bait. They usually feed off the bottom and prefer clear water, but they can live with slightly muddy conditions. A good fighter, the drum can please light tackle anglers right on through the hottest summers. Their meat is solid and makes excellent tablefare.

Smelt are small, slender bodied fish that provide much forage for Lake Ontario gamefish. They are good eating for people, too, and are eagerly sought, mainly by dip netters. In Lake Ontario, these fish are readily accessible when trying to spawn immediately after ice out. They are caught in tributaries at night by anglers using a light or lantern and a dip net; most are netted up tributaries within two miles of the lake. Smelt can be taken in any number, at any time during the entire year. However, after this early season action, they go very deep in the lake and just aren't pursued by sportfishermen.

MORE ON DOWNRIGGERS & ELECTRONICS

"Fishermen were fast to embrace this potent new device, and trout-less summers quickly gave way to more and more trout and eventually salmon being piled up."

11

Today's fishermen are lucky indeed to be able to fish for and catch trout and salmon year round. Not too many years ago, anglers would annually hang up their tackle during the sultry summer season. Not only was trolling with wire or lead core line unsporting, but it produced spotty results. Fishermen knew that the deeper the fish went, the progressively heavier the tackle became. And the heavier the tackle, of course, the less enjoyable the sport. Thus, until the advent of the downrigger, many fished bait or jigged for trout during the summer, or, often, didn't fish at all (unless he was after bass, pike, or panfish, which remain readily available all summer near shore).

Not only did the advent of the downrigger allow the fisherman to use more sporting fishing tackle, but it also allowed him to troll through more fish feeding areas than would have been physically possible by any other means. With a downrigger, line as light as four pound test can effectively be used to catch trout down over 120 feet deep. Fishermen were fast to embrace this potent new device, and troutless summers quickly gave way to more and more trout and eventually salmon being piled up on the docks around the lake.

TYPES OF DOWNRIGGERS
Over the years, we have used many downriggers for all sorts of fishing around the Great Lakes. There are essentially two types. The first is the manual kind, which has a hand crank to raise or lower the trolling weight (this weight will vary from 6-10 pounds in either the Cannon Ball or Fish styles). The other is totally electric, and only a switch is needed to raise or lower the trolling weight. The automatic downriggers are much more convenient, and expectedly, more expensive. Beside manual or motor, you should be aware of several other features that are very popular and often used by those who consistently catch fish.

Make certain that each downrigger you buy has some sort of a digital display; some are computerized, others are clicked by the turning spool. Such displays indicate exactly how deep the trolling weight is. This information will allow you to get the weights to the depth where fish are indicated on the fish finder unit (more on this later in this chapter). Also, make certain that at least one downrigger unit has a thermal couplet or probe attached to it, so that

Although manufacturer designs vary, many downrigger components are universal. Here is a list and description of them:

1. Manual Handle — Attached to reel, rotated to release or regain cable. Electric downriggers do not have handles.
2. Reel — A rotating wheel capable of holding 600 feet of cable.
3. Drag — System that allows line to come off downrigger reel if the weights entangle on some bottom obstacle.
4. Cable — Stainless steel wire, up to 150 pound test, often with attached thermal sensing cable.
5. Extension of Arm — Device used to hold cable out away from the boat. Come in a variety of lengths.
6. Guide Wheel — Allows cable to pass through it at the end of the extension.
7. Mount — Location where the downrigger is attached to the boat. Are swivel mounted for operational ease.
8. Digital Counter — Device used to count the number of feet the trolling weight is down.
9. Weight — 6, 8, 10, or 12 pound weight (often cannon balls) used to pull cable down. Come in different colors, often used as attractors.
10. Release Mechanism — Attached to cable or weight, the release is responsible for allowing the fish to pull the line free of the cable.
11. Rod Holder — Often single or double, allows you to fish one or more rods off one downrigger.

▶ *11a. FISHING WITH DOWNRIGGERS — Basic Components*

you will be able to see the exact temperature at the depth recorded on the digital depth recorder. These devices are very important and their added cost well justified. For the day in, day out fisherman, we have used and can recommend any of the following dependable downriggers:

1. Cannon. Their catalog lists both manual and automatic models. All have excellent swivel mounts, rod holders and various boom lengths, and all are extremely durable.
2. Penn. Fathom-Master downriggers, capable of getting down 10-600' or anywhere in between. Available in six, hand cranked models with a 25-inch or 48-inch boom and rod holder capabilities.

Cannon has been among the leaders in downrigger equipment

3. Luhr-Jensen. Trac II & Trac III short and long arm series with both manual crank and "Auto-Electric." Swivel base of nylon, heavy anodized aluminum and stainless steel construction with attached rod holders.
4. Big John. Downriggers and Mini Riggers, some styles featuring manual cranks and others totally electric. Trolling weights to 12 pounds. Extremely lightweight.
5. Riviera. New Generation Downriggers, with manual or electric featuring clutch release, full 360 degree swivel base, chip and peel inhibiting paint, stronger weather resistant Lexan reel for longer life, stainless steel cable, rod holders, and extension arm screws designed not to loosen from vibrations.
6. Proos. Quality down-trollers, with all-metal rugged design, smooth operating deep water design, ridged lock holed aluminum reels. Baked-on wrinkle coat looks good and lasts; choice of fixed or swivel heads. Limited warranty at no extra charge, plus choice of manual or motor drive with slip clutch.

RELEASE MECHANISMS

Besides the basic unit, an important area of concern is the release mechanism used in conjunction with the downrigger. This device is responsible for keeping the lure in place behind the downrigger cable. Once a fish strikes the lure, the mechanism must flawlessly release the line so that the angler above knows that there's a fish on the line. Should the mechanism fail to release the line, a big fish could snap the lure right off and be on his way. Therefore, only use the best release mechanisms and service them well to keep them in top notch working order throughout the year.

There are many types of release mechanisms on the market. Some are called "quick" releases, and others work as simply as placing a button with the line running through it into a spring so that when the fish strikes, it pulls the button out and the line is set free of the spring. However, two of the better releases on the market today are the "Black" and "Roemer" releases. Each of these can be stacked on your downrigger cable giving you the capability of fishing more than one rod per downrigger and at different depths.

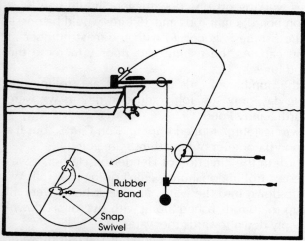

Rubber Band

Snap Swivel

▶ *11b. DOWNRIGGER TACTICS: ONE ROD TWO LURES — Two lures can be trolled effectively off one rod. Use a snap swivel and a rubber band to hold the upper lure in place. Once a fish strikes, the rubber band will break or slide along with the swivel to the second lure. Now you can strike and reel in the fish.*

Of course, the more lines fished off a downrigger or the deeper you go, the heavier the downrigger weight required.

STACKING RELEASE MECHANISMS

To stack your lures, use several release mechanisms placed one on top of the other (stacked) on the downrigger cable. Using a downrigger which has two rod holders attached to it, place the line from one rod into the bottom release. Loosen the drag on the reel, run the lure off behind, and run the trolling weight down 6-8 feet into the water while allowing the cable to slide through the other release mechanism which you hold in your hand. Now, either run a second lure off the first line (see Fig. 11-b) or run the line from the second rod to the upper release device. Again, you can place a second lure on this line at this point after running the weight down a few feet more. Now, loosen the second drag and lower the weight and lure into position at the required depth.

Once in position, adjust the drags to proper working strength. Then, take up line by cranking the reels until the rods display a big bend and the line is rather taut. Once done, you will have between two and four lures working off one downrigger. Should you have four downriggers on board, eight rods and 16 lures would be possible. However, if the fishing is good, go with the least number of rods and lures you can. As the fishing gets poorer, increase the number of rods and lures.

"Judging from the number of rods these boats are trolling, it's going to be a long day," my son John said one day as we were heading out of North Sandy Pond.

"I hope you're wrong John," replied Captain Ron Clark, "but it's usually a pretty good barometer of how things are going."

As we swung north in the direction of Henderson Harbor, it was obvious that the boats trolling offshore weren't doing too well. We rarely saw a net dip down into the water, and most boats were all decked out with up to 10 rods fished along with five or six downriggers all bent deeply down towards the water.

"These guys are fishing for lakers suspended in 140 feet of water. Things have been pretty slow down this way, but we should find it a little different off Stony Point," the captain added.

The ride to Stony Point took about 25 minutes. On the way, my two sons, John and Steven, and Mike Kersey readied the five rods we were about to use.

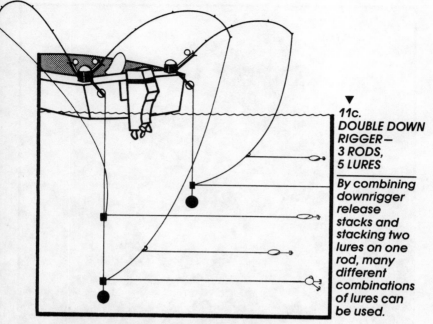

▼
**11c.
DOUBLE DOWN
RIGGER –
3 RODS,
5 LURES**

By combining
downrigger
release
stacks and
stacking two
lures on one
rod, many
different
combinations
of lures can
be used.

"I feel better already. We're only going to use five rods," John quipped.

"Not so fast," said the captain. "There's five more stashed away in the cabin just in case."

When using from 5-10 rods, you must be constantly aware of how deep each rod is and exactly how far down the bottom is. One thing you don't want to happen out there is for your downrigger weights to bounce along the bottom where they can get stuck. To avoid this, the moment it's obvious that the bottom is rising, start the deepest weights up first.

The hedge against failing to get the lures up in time is the drag incorporated into the better downriggers. This is just like the drag on a fishing reel. Rather than have a snagged cable pull taut and break, the drag simply allows more cable to pull off the downrigger cable reel itself. This gives you enough time to turn your boat around and attempt to pull the snagged lures off the bottom while going in the opposite direction.

Another device that consistently equates to limit catches of trout and salmon is a good fish finder. It's a hard and cold fact: You can troll all day, but if you don't know how deep the fish are, it's very easy to catch the skunk. With a fish finder, you'll quickly

see where the fish are and put all your lures down at that depth. You may still come back fishless, but your chances of success will have improved dramatically.

With a good fish finder and a navigational chart, locating lake trout and salmon in 140 feet of water can be done. With a paper graph recorder, color video "chromograph," and the lead crystal recorder, accurate visualizations of the bottom and any fish in between can be made and relayed to the fishermen above.

HOW A FISH FINDER WORKS

The first time we used a fish finder on Lake Ontario was quite an experience. On our graph recorder we quickly saw some spine tingling marks that looked like they had to be submarines. When the first rod popped up, our hearts almost stopped.

All these recorders work by electronically measuring the time it takes for sound waves to travel from the top of the water to the bottom and then back again. The sound waves leave a transducer, which is usually mounted through the hull of the boat, and travel downward bouncing off the bottom or anything, like fish, in between. All chart recorders have four major components: a control center, a transmitter, a receiver, and a recording screen.

You supply information such as paper speed, depth of reading required, and perhaps lightness or darkness of image. The control center directs the transmitter to send signals downward through the transducer in a pattern which resembles a cone. All returning signals are received in the transducer and sent to the receiver. A picture is then displayed on the scene where it can be viewed (chromograph and lead crystal), or recorded permanently on paper. These are the basic functions of the recorder or fish finder, though some companies have made modifications to their receivers. For example, Humminbird has developed a less expensive new Lead Crystal Recorder which has far fewer receiving blocks on its screen. Thus images are blunt, more like a flasher, but you can see the bottom and the fish in between. Also, some recorders show a color TV screen (Chromograph) where all things appear in slightly different colors or tones.

With information provided by the recorders, smart fishermen formulate plans to zero in on the different species found around the lake. For example, if all the blips (a blip indicates a fish) are registering down about 40 feet in 56-60 degrees of water, the fishermen should make the deduction that the species is probably brown trout. If down 120 feet in 51 degrees of water, the fish will most likely be lake trout. Therefore, during the day, you should be fishing the layer of water associated with the species you intend to catch. As the evening approaches, any big blips found near the bottom in 140 feet or more of water (probably at a temperature around 48 degrees though temperature is not too critical here) should be chinook salmon.

INTEGRATING SYSTEMS

Since this deep water trolling is the most difficult, let's take a closer look at it and see how you can integrate systems for maximum effectiveness.

Late in July, boats fishing out of Olcott and Wilson encounter salmon in deep water. They troll squids and spoons from 4 PM until dusk (the prime time). This is real deep trolling and it can be tricky! For example, you may be recording fish at 145 feet. So, you let your trolling weights down to 140 feet deep. However, since your forward speed will put a considerable drag on the weights, they will rise up in the water, and they will not be down 140 feet. In order to get those weights to the required depth, the following calculations must be made. By knowing the forward speed of the boat and by measuring the angle at which the downrigger cable enters the water, you can figure how much extra cable must be payed out. For example, if a boat traveling at 2.5 mph has its cables entering the water at 45 degrees, it would take about 195 feet of cable to reach 140 feet; for 30 degrees, 170 feet; and for 15 degrees, about 155 feet (see Fig. 12-b).

Armed with this knowledge, you watch the fish finder and the moment fish appear on the screen, you take note of their depth. Then, you assess what type of fish they probably are. Each fish should be trolled at a different speed (see Fig. 12-a). Now, you adjust the speed of your boat to the species, select the associated lures, and plan a good lure mix and pattern.

SETTING A TROLLING PATTERN

To figure out how much cable to let out, apply the depth of the fish shown on your fish finder to the downrigger settings found in Fig. 12-b. Now, start setting up your pattern. For an example, turn back to Ch.7 and Fig. 7-b. Here you see six rods with four downriggers pulling eight lures through the water. The left rigger has two rods stacked one above the other on two different releases. The upper release has a rod that has two lures stacked on the same line, and so on.

When trolling in shallow water, run your lures back between 30-100 feet. As your weights go deeper, the distance that you drop your lures back can be decreased. Eventually, when fishing very deep, your lures may only be back from 10-20 feet.

Another situation may arise: what do you do if all your riggers are down deep and a fish strikes one? Should you reel them all up? After all, it may have taken some time and effort to set up a complex pattern. Must you break that pattern down the moment a fish strikes? Well, the answer is that you should keep your boat going as slow as possible in a forward direction. The other lures can be left down in pattern as long as the hooked fish isn't too big and fights his way up to the surface well behind the other lures.

If, however, you have hooked a big fish and there's a possibility that it may run through the other lures, you should set about bringing them up as quickly as possible. No one said it was going to be easy!

KEEP IN TOUCH BY VHF RADIO

Finally, most sailors on Lake Ontario have some means of radio communications: Either a simple CB radio or a VHF Marine Radio system. With one of these, you can monitor conversations between successful fishermen, keep in touch with friends on other craft, monitor lake weather reports, or signal if in trouble. With a radio, you're never alone. Without it, you're out of touch and in a less comfortable position in regard to the weather.

I hope that you now have a better feel for the electronics used on the lake, and that you can see how an integrated system will lead to more fish in the box. In the next two chapters we're going to put much of this information to use.

SUMMER TROLLING

"Mike grabbed the rod, pointed it toward the water and began reeling. When he reared back, his big rod curled up like a pretzel!"

12

Fishing for trout and salmon during the long, blistering hot days of summer, July and August, means fishing deep. Although, the weather cooperates, making boating and fishing easy, putting trout and salmon into the fish box is no easy matter. The lake trout are the quickest to cooperate and the most commonly sought of the cold water species during this season. Their preferred temperature zone is typically down 70 feet or more, making the only practical way to fish for them with downriggers. Unfortunately for surf casters, once the thermocline moves this deep the chance of trout or salmon from shore is even more remote than in late spring.

Along with the lake trout, brown trout can still be caught inshore (inshore meaning within a few miles). Also, because of the large scale salmon stocking programs conducted by both New York State and Canada, more and more juvenile chinook and coho (fish from 5-15 pounds) are showing up in deep-water summer catches. However, fishing still remains best for the eager lake trout.

CATCHING SUSPENDED LAKE TROUT

It is during the summer, when their preferred temperature is very deep, that lake trout uncharacteristically suspend. No one knows exactly why they move up from the bottom, but it may be because the bait has moved offshore. Whatever the explanation, they can most often be found between 70-100 feet. When fishing in deeper water, keep your lures where the water temperature is reading 49-51 degrees (somewhere between 40-70 feet above the bottom) and maintain a 2 MPH forward speed.

Small boat fishermen can find this depth in as close as 1½ to 2 miles offshore. Even though this is a short distance and the weather may be sunny and warm, you must remain ever alert and keep a constant watch out for summer squalls and thunderstorms. They can sneak up on you in minutes and turn the lake into an ugly sea. Make certain to have enough boat and horsepower under you to get quickly and safely back to the nearest inlet.

One hotspot during the summer season is Henderson Harbor by Stony Point. Here, 49-51 degrees of water is found around 100 feet deep (as mentioned in Ch. 8). This depth coincides perfectly with underwater canyons and cliffs, which give large lakers the exact temperature and structure they need (here they don't suspend). Two methods you can try on these fish are vertical jigging (see Ch. 8) or trolling.

MID SUMMER TROLLING TECHNIQUES

During the mid summer period, trolling hardware remains pretty much the same. From this point on, we'll assume that you have one or more reputable downriggers and a good fish finder and that you're ready to arm yourself with a good selection of effective lures. Naturally, you'll also want to know the best approaches for presenting these lures to the lake trout.

Speed (MPH)		Species	Speed (MPH)		Species
Spring Fall	2¼ - 3 3 - 4	Chinook	Spring Fall	2 - 2½ 2¼ - 3¼	Rainbows & Browns
Spring Fall	2 - 2¾ 2½ - 3¼	Coho	Spring Fall	1 - 1¾ 1½ - 2¼	Lake Trout
Sum Fall	2 - 2½	Walleyes	Clear Water Unclear Water	5 - 6 3 - 5	Muskies

▶ *12a. TROLLING SPEEDS*

For best results while trolling summer lake trout, use flutter spoons and chartreuse swimming plugs either stacked on one or two rods or in combinations of the two (see Fig. 7-b). It is best to fish the flutter spoon about eight feet above the swimming plug. Attach the spoon back at the end of a six-foot leader. This leader is placed on the fishing line with a snap swivel and held in place with a rubber band. When a fish strikes the spoon, the rubber band will either break or slide down the line along with the snap swivel. Once the snap swivel reaches the swivel attached to the crankbait, it can't go any further and the fish is reeled in. The plug should be 10 feet behind its release mechanism (about 8 feet below the spoon). You can also troll flies and flash squids alone or behind swimming plugs or dodgers (see Figs. 8-f, 13-a).

Should things get slow, try pulling some lures through 56-60 degrees of water for brown trout. This water temperature is usually down around 40 feet, well above the lakers. Also, if while fishing for the lake trout you get a false strike (that is, a fish pulls a lure out of the release mechanism, but isn't hooked), reel the lure back to the surface slowly in hopes of catching a brown or something that may be swimming in another temperature zone above where the false strike occurred.

Although the brown trout are available, they're so well spread out that fishing for them is often very difficult. However, with the introduction of the "Skamania" steelhead rainbow trout, a void may soon be filled along the shoreline during this period. The Skamania steelhead are considered to be a warm water species of trout and should thus remain in close to shore during the summer.

TROLLING LURE SELECTIONS

Some relatively new trolling lures that have already proven their worth are put out by Storm Lures. Their Thinfin Shad is a tremendous trout catcher in any lake or reservoir sporting a sizable population of alewife herring. Their Wiggle Wart and Wee Wart also have proven very effective on smallmouth bass inshore and steelhead rainbow trout offshore. The best finish for the ThinFin Shad often seems to be silver, while the Warts are better in hot colors like Fluorescent Red and Chartreuse.

From Luhr-Jensen, the Alpena Diamond is an old standby. This heavy spoon has caught more than its share of lakers and salmon. A new lure put out now by this company for this kind of fishing is their Flutterspoon. Hammered Nickel, Brass and Nickel, Nickel/Neon Blue Stripe, and Silver Plate all are hailing lake trout well in Lake Ontario. Another entry is their Loco. However, if you use this lure, replace the set of trebles with a single salmon type hook. The Chartreuse Dot and Nickle/Silver Prism-lite are two other good producing patterns.

From Mann's Company, we get the Chartreuse Finn Mann and Hackelback lures. These lures have proven to be two of the best fish attractors and catchers. On the best days we have encountered on Lake Ontario, these lures always seemed to be part of our pattern.

If you can keep your lures spread out in the section or level of water displaying the 51 degree temperature, you will catch more fish. Should one depth prove to be more productive, quickly place more lures at that depth. If fish are registering on your recorder and you're not being too successful, the first thing you do is try to slow your boat down! Then, if still unsuccessful, change lure patterns and lure combinations. As a last resort move to a new area.

BIG CHINOOK MOVE INSHORE

As the summer progresses, more small chinook, coho, and land-locked salmon begin showing up in daily catches. Also, around the end of July, start looking for big chinook and coho salmon to be caught. These big chinook are first caught somewhere along the southern tier between 1-3 miles offshore in about 140 feet of water. Unlike the lake trout that suspend during much of this period, the kings are caught right on the bottom.

If you intend to fish for these early salmon, plan to be out at an early hour. King salmon are very light sensitive. Once the sun is high in the sky, they head for the bottom (deeper than 140 feet) and tend to get lost. Only as evening approaches do they come closer to shore (140 feet of water or less) to feed. A second feeding takes place from about 3 AM until about an hour after daybreak.

To try and help you understand more about the tackle, lures and approaches used during this period, and to review some of what has already been discussed in this chapter, follow Mike Kersey and myself as we pursue a typical mid summer afternoon fishing for bass and salmon along the southern tier.

Mike and I were fishing for smallmouth bass in the Niagara River one day late in July when he turned to me and said, "We better head back to the Fort (Niagara), it's about that time." Without hesitation, the engine on our 20 foot Wellcraft was engaged and we raced back to the public launch ramp. As soon as the boat was out of the water, Mike cleaned the bass and I readied the boat for the short trip to Olcott.

"I hope the reports are right," Mike said. "It's probably too early, but if the chinook are showing up, we've got to be there!"

After arriving in Olcott, about 18 miles east of the fort, we traveled down Main Street where we put the boat into Eighteen Mile Creek. It was now 3 PM and we could see other anglers returning to the ramp and unloading some salmon and steelhead. It didn't appear to be a slaughter, but Mike and I couldn't help wondering if we had come too late in the day.

After checking fuel, ice, and tackle, we fired the engine and headed due north along the river. There were fishermen working the piers which protected the entrance of the harbor, and there was a large crane on a barge doing some dredging work. Once through the inlet, we opened up the engine and headed offshore.

As Mike tied on some 17-pound test leader, a ball-bearing coastlock swivel, and heavy duty barrel swivel, I turned the fish finder unit on. We continued due north until we sighted several boats further offshore trolling deep water slightly east of where we were heading. Pointing at the boats, I called to Mike, "I bet they're fishing the 140 foot line."

Within minutes, we were about as far offshore as the little fleet that was slowly trolling to our east. The recorder indicated that we were in 130 feet of water. We reduced our forward speed down to 3 MPH, which is perfect for salmon during the summer, and began preparing the downriggers.

"My guess is we're about 2 miles out. Let's continue heading

Desired Depth (Feet)	Angle At Which Your Downrigger Cable Enters The Water		
	15°	30°	45°
10	10	12	14
20	22	24	28
30	32	35	42
40	42	46	56
50	52	58	70
60	62	68	84
70	72	80	98
80	83	92	110
90	93	104	125
100	104	115	140
110	115	127	155
120	125	138	170
130	135	150	180
140	146	160	195
150	156	170	210

(Vertical label: Amount Of Downrigger Cable You Must Let Out To Reach Desired Depth)

▶ 12b. DOWNRIGGER SETTINGS—This is a general guideline! Speed, current, winds, and weight size all affect these figures.

offshore until we meet the 140 foot line. Then, we'll turn and head west," I said to Mike.

"Good," he replied, "we can listen to the radio and see if these guys are doing anything. If they are, we won't be too far away."

"Right," I added as Mike readied to lower the first squid which was about 15 feet behind the release mechanism.

With big chinook salmon the target, we were fishing 17 pound test tackle all the way! We were also using only one lure per rod and one rod per downrigger. Therefore, we planned to run 4 lures down around 125 feet. Our downrigger setting card indicated that with a 30 degree angle we had to let out 160 feet of cable to get down 125 feet. As our downrigger weights descended, we watched them on the recorder. About 100 feet down, they disappeared from the screen.

We ran two squids and two spoons at the end of 160 feet of cable. One squid was green, and the other was a black and yellow combination. The first spoon was a chartreuse Scalelite Wobbler and the second was a fluorescent red Coho Flasher. Because of the extreme depth, we opted not to use "Dodgers" in front of any of the lures. They would serve only to increase the drag and cause us to pay out more cable.

Keeping an eye on the recorder, we noticed good schools of bait-fish down around 120 feet. This was a good sign. After perhaps five minutes of trolling, we were directly over the 140 foot line. I eased the boat west, and Mike adjusted the downriggers. Using our topo-graphic map, I planned to travel north until we hit a drop-off into 160 feet of water about 5 miles further on.

The temperature down at 135 feet was a chilly 49 degrees. It fluctuated as high as 51 degrees, but remained right around the 49 degree mark. An hour passed and we hadn't recorded a single fish on the machine nor had we heard about any immediate action over the radio.

"There's no reason to change lures," I called to Mike as he started one up off the bottom.

"I'm not changing," came his reply, "I'm just checking its action."

With that, a second 9 foot rod sprung up! "There's one Mike," I yelled as he raced for the limp rod!

Mike grabbed the rod, pointed it toward the water and began reeling. When he reared back, his big rod curled up like a pretzel.

"It feels like a beauty!"

I tended to the other rods as Mike fought the fish. Within about 15 minutes, Mike had a nice, fat 17 pound chinook begging to be netted.

"Well, I guess they're here," came his smiling reply.

We set up again, but didn't get another strike. Later that evening, we checked our paper from the recorder. You know, there wasn't a single blip recorded on it down below 100 feet. The big salmon had taken the lure off the recorder. We never saw him. Nor did we see any others. However, talking with other guys who were pulling their boats out of the water near us proved that the 140 foot depth was where all the action was. And without a recorder, it would have been almost impossible to have found and fished it. So, even though our unit didn't get to record any fish, it did make all the difference; and better yet, we knew that we'd be heading back to the same location the next day!

While trolling deep water, one thing became perfectly clear. Although we were using proper downrigger settings, we had to do much experimenting to make certain that we were down near the bottom. The settings were a good guide, but they were rarely right! This was perhaps due to the fact that we had to read the entry angle of our line into the water. If we read the angle wrong, then our calculations were wrong. Therefore, we devised this way to get near the bottom: Using the settings, we would lower our first downrigger to which was attached a Countdown Rapala (deep running) plug. Since this plug would swim beneath the trolling weight, we continued to lower the weight slowly, until the plug hit the bottom and pulled free of the release. We then checked the depth recorded on the dial and fished all our other riggers five feet above that depth. We also removed the Countdown Rapala and replaced it with another salmon lure.

Trolling deep water is difficult, but with the aid of a good fish finder, downriggers, and a topographic map, it isn't impossible. Our experiences off Olcott that summer taught us much, but we still couldn't wait for the fish to move in. When they did, we headed for the Bay of Mexico, and the heart-stopping action described in the next chapter.

TROLLING GIANT SALMON

"Late August is a time of great excitement on the great lake. When those monstrous chinooks move inshore prior to spawning, all hell breaks loose!"

13

Late August is a time of great excitement on the big lake. When those monstrous chinook salmon move inshore, all hell breaks loose! These tackle busters, ranging from 15-45 pounds, can keep an angler at the rod for an hour or more, while making one spectacular run after another.

Once while fishing with outdoor writer Ron Jacobsen, Captain Jack Baker and his mate Deborah Somers aboard the Chinook II, we had three chinook salmon hook-ups in one day while actually fishing for brown and lake trout in Mexico Bay. The salmon took Sutton 88 spoons and a green flash squid trailed 16 inches behind a Chrome, 8-inch Abe & Al Flasher at about 2.5 MPH. We were on the water at 6 AM trolling west out of the river headed for the Nine Mile Point Nuclear Power Complex. We managed to catch several lake trout and browns before the first chinook struck, somewhere around 9 AM in the morning.

NO MISTAKING A CHINOOK

The strike of a chinook is distinct! Once the big fish is hooked, the line will come steadily off the spool of your reel against its drag as the powerful fish heads away from the boat. A deep fighter, chinook are often very hard to get up away from the bottom. Usually, one long deep run is made which may peel off 300 yards of line or more . . . and it may be coming off a reel that has been designed to hold perhaps 240 yards of line (typically 14-17 pound test). How then, you may ask, does anyone ever land a chinook? The answer is rather simple. Once it has been determined that you have a big chinook on, those around you must reel in all the other rods and crank up all the downrigger weights to get them out of your way. The boat is then put into gear and run on an angle toward the big fish. Rod tension is maintained, while precious line is recaptured.

After enough line has been gained back, the boat should be turned perpendicular to the fish. The fish should then be allowed to continue his run, or make a second run against the full strength of the drag (not a tight drag). Should the chinook prove to be a giant, you may have to chase the fish again, though usually, a second such maneuver isn't necessary.

With the fish still over 150 yards away, there's plenty of anticipation and adrenalin flowing as the lucky angler applies the pressure and brings the big fish ever closer to the boat.

Often these huge chinooks will clear the water with electrifying leaps. At other times, they may charge right at the boat. The latter happened one time on a charter I was on.

"I think I lost him," cried Debbie as the big rod she was holding straightened up out of its deep bow.

"Reel fast," coached Captain Jack, "the fish may still be on and headed for the boat!"

"No, he's gone, I don't feel anything," exclaimed Debbie.

With that, it dawned on her that by now she should have at least felt the lure, but she wasn't feeling anything at all. The fish had to be headed right for the boat! Debbie quickly ducked the tip of her rod down deep into the water and as she did, she screamed, "he's still there!" Wisely, she brought the throbbing rod under the propeller and up on the other side of the boat. A big smile beamed across her deeply suntanned face as she continued to fight what turned out to be her biggest salmon ever: A 27-pound chinook!

So go the happy stories of August, September, and October, when the modus operandi is shallow water trolling for giant chinook salmon. A big bruiser, the chinook requires special tackle and trolling know-how in order to get him to strike, and then to get him in. Often, attention to detail makes the difference between a successful day with several strikes and a fish or two, and a day that hasn't been too productive. The story of chinook and coho salmon actually begins a few years before and in the spring.

Salmon that have been reared in the hatchery are released in their smolt stage (4-7 inches long) during the spring into many rivers and tributaries. They migrate out into Lake Ontario under the cover of darkness when the river water temperature has risen to between 44-50 degrees. Movement from these rivers may occur quickly, but usually takes between 2-3 weeks. The diet of these smolt salmon consists primarily of aquatic insects, small fish, and salmon fry.

Once in the big lake, dietary considerations remain pretty much the same until the fish reach a pound or two. Then, alewife herring and smelt become the major staples. Stomach content surveys conducted by state biologists during fishing contests find most chinook and coho stomachs to be either empty or containing a high percentage of the above mentioned forage species. The reason many have empty stomachs may be that the fish regurgitate while

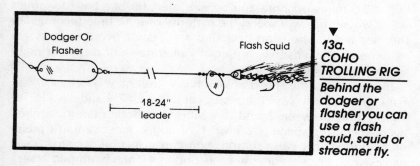

Dodger Or Flasher

Flash Squid

18-24" leader

▼
13a. COHO TROLLING RIG
Behind the dodger or flasher you can use a flash squid, squid or streamer fly.

fighting for their lives or that they haven't eaten for a day or more while searching for baitfish.

PHENOMENAL GROWTH RATES

Growth rates for these yearling smolt are phenomenal. At 1½ years of age, the fish range from 3-10 pounds with the average somewhere around 6 pounds. For 2½ year olds, the range is 10-26 pounds, with the average 17 pounds. At this point, the cohos return in mass to spawn, while the chinook remain out in the lake to feed for another year.

At the end of 3½ years, the sexually mature chinook weigh from 15-32 pounds, with the average fish tipping the scales in the neighborhood of 24 pounds. In 4½ years, they range between 25-45 pounds and average near 32 pounds, while a 5½ year old will approach 50 pounds. During these years, the adult chinook may enter the river of its origin (where it was planted by the hatchery), spawn, and die. The present rod & reel record for the lake stands at 47 pounds, which is also a Great Lakes Record. The Lake Ontario and New York State record coho weighed 30 pounds 12 ounces.

During the spring, one year old "jack" chinook and coho salmon weighing from 3-6 pounds come in close to shore and are caught along with the brown trout. Although they aren't taken in any great numbers, nearly every limit of fish this time of year has a few jack salmon mixed in. These fish, especially the cohos, are very edible!

Although on occasion adult chinook or coho salmon are caught along with the ice-out browns, for the most part ice-out trolling is done along the shore and the larger salmon usually remain well offshore and relatively unmolested. If you want to find them, troll about 3-5 miles offshore and be ever alert for patches of warmer water where they will spend the majority of their time feeding. For the best results, troll on days that are heavily overcast (they are extremely light sensitive), especially near dawn or dusk (for night fishing see Ch. 14).

In the spring, the speed at which you troll may also be critical. For chinooks, troll swimming plugs at between 2¼ and 3 MPH. For cohos, troll between 2 and 2¾ MPH. For both salmon, a good average starting speed is 2.5 MPH. Although most captains prefer plugs during this early season, you can also troll spoons. Some early season favorites are the Loco, Sutton 44, and Northport Nailer.

THE PHANTOMS OF SUMMER
As summer approaches, the chinook and coho salmon seem to disappear from the lake. Rarely do they show up in catches made by trollers working even miles offshore, and they're even less common inshore. Research on this fascinating subject is ongoing, and several theories have been proposed as to the whereabouts of summer salmon. Here are some of them.

1. The Deep Hole Theory. According to this line of thinking, salmon during the summer remain very deep in the lake, where there's enough oxygen to support them. They only rise up out of this "hole" to feed heavily early in the morning near dawn, and again late in the afternoon near dusk and on into the night. Since more angler effort is extended during the day, there would be far less overall opportunity to make contact with the feeding salmon.

2. The Deep Current Theory. With an eye to the strong migratory tendencies of salmon, this theory holds that during the summer the fish may go down deep into the lake's well oxygenated currents. In some cases they may travel unnoticed in these currents at 300 feet of depth or more. Since little is known about the deep currents in the lake, it would be difficult to try and find them and the fish that supposedly follow them.

3. The Forage Theory. This view, as proposed by Dr. Mike Voiland, Sea Grant specialist at SUNY Brockport and the skipper of the education vessel Ontario, suggests that baitfish (or forage) have a strong affect on the behavior of salmon in Lake Ontario.

Since alewifes and smelt (the baitfish) are available in large numbers ranging in depths down to 200 feet, the salmon in summer may not only be very deep but very full. These factors — combined with the dawn and dusk feeding hours — make it very difficult to catch or even detect the salmon.

4. The Dispersion Or Density Theory. Since the salmon can range over a wide territory in a short period of time, Dr. Jim Haynes, biologist at SUNY Brockport and Sea Grant researcher suggests that they may scatter throughout the depths of the basin only coming together in front of tributaries just before spawning time. This lack of concentration makes it difficult to catch a great number of salmon during the summer.

5. Deep Water And Temperature Theory. Many captains, myself included, feel that many of the above theories are true at least in part. The dispersion, along with the availability of bait and the selective feeding hours account for the low return of these great fighting fish during the summer. However, the salmon are there in the lake and can be caught. This theory contends that the fish go down as deep as 300 feet or more, where there's oxygen (Current Theory) and feed in relative seclusion in water with a temperature ranging from 42-52 degrees. Since this temperature is well below their more usual inshore preference of 52-54 degrees, few captains fish this deep or even focus their depth finders this deep in the summer. Therefore, the salmon go virtually undetected and uncaught.

If you buy this last theory, you may now understand why in the last chapter we suggested trolling in 140 feet of water and stated that the 49-degree water temperature found there (below the usual salmon norm) should not be a problem. If the theory has merit, the 49-degree mark would be just above the temperature at which they spend the majority of their summer.

The thing that actually triggers the inshore movement of the salmon in mid-summer is the amount of daylight. As the season wears on, days become progressively shorter. This decrease in daylight sometime in late July or early August awakens the ancient salmon instinct to begin moving inshore, there to prepare for a final journey up a river in search of a suitable place to spawn.

Although some juvenile salmon not mature enough to spawn fol-

▶ *King salmon aren't the only monsters in Lake Ontario. Cohos, like this brute, have been taken in excess of 30 pounds.*

low the larger migraters inshore, very few actually follow them into the rivers. Once inshore, the big salmon consistently hold in 52-54 degrees of water making everyone trolling for them intent on fishing this exact water temperature. Unfortunately, many come to believe that this is the only temperature at which salmon can be caught, at any time.

FANTASTIC INSHORE ACTION

Once the salmon move inshore, chinook ranging from 10-32 pounds and coho ranging from 6-20 pounds can be expected to remain for a while in front of the major spawning tributaries. As stated earlier, you will most assuredly find them near the Niagara River, the Genesee River, the Oswego River, the Salmon River, and the Black River. They will usually be in water that is 40-80 feet deep, shows a temperature of 52-54 degrees Fahrenheit, and is within a mile of the beach. Look for the chinook salmon to register as isolated big blips very near the bottom. Smaller, more closely packed blips anywhere in this temperature range usually indicate cohos.

If you can get this act together, you will score heavily on big salmon from mid-August on into October. The tackle requirements are still the same: trolling rods to nine feet long and reels capable of holding 250 yards of 17 pound test line. This in addition to a wide variety of lures including spoons, plugs, and squids in assorted sizes and colors; a large-framed and sturdy landing net; and an assortment of dodgers and flashers in different sizes and colors.

On one such trip late in August several years ago, I was trolling with Capt. Ron Clark out of Sandy Pond, N.Y., Andy Gennaro and my two sons, John and Steven. Our combined catch included 15 coho salmon to 15 pounds, several brown trout to 8 pounds, several lake trout to 11 pounds, and a 22 pound chinook salmon! On that day, we could read many big blips while we were about a half mile off the Salmon River mouth in about 50 feet of water at 54 degrees. However, these fish wouldn't strike. So we maintained good reference on their location and trolled away from them, getting into schools of more cooperative coho salmon and brown trout.

We picked away at the schools of smaller fish, but every once in a while pulled some lures through the area where we found the larger blips. On one such turn, a big chinook finally decided to take. After about a 10 minute struggle, it succeeded in pulling free, but we were then confident that the chinooks would soon be feeding. It wasn't long after that we tied into and caught our 22 pounder after a battle of about 20 minutes.

The moral is to be persistent in your efforts during late summer. Troll at slightly faster speeds (2.5-4 MPH), and remember that these fish will feed sooner or later. Even though you have them in shallow water and in full view on your fish finder it doesn't guarantee that they will hit. Keep trying until they do.

SPECIFIC GEAR TO USE
Some of the trolling plugs that we have used at this time of year and can recommend are: Fire Plugs; Hot Shots; J-Plugs; Lucky Louies; Lindy Pop-Tails; Tiger Plugs; and Northport Nailers. Best colors include blue/silver, green/yellow, chartreuse, and chartreuse red dot. Sizes should range from 4-6 inches or ½ to 2 ounces.

For spoons, the following have brought success: Sutton #31, #44, and #88HT; Flutter-Lite; Flutter Spoon; Evil Eye; L.G. Johnson; Coho Flasher; two-colored spoons like the Pine Valley and Northern flutterspoons; Red Eye Wiggler; Alpena Diamond; Hopkin's Shorty; and Krocodile. In addition, you should invest in some different colored Prism Tape. If you are offshore and would like to try a different colored lure, all you have to do is take the one you are already using and cover it with the Prism Tape of your choice. "Presto!" You have a "new" lure.

For trolling squids (often called flies), try to get some that are termed "Flash Squids." This is a squid that has a spinner blade in front of it. The flashing blade adds a lifelike feature to the lure and often increases its effectiveness. There are many squids on the market, among them: Mai Tai; Seducer; Luhr Jensen's Twinkle and Skimpy Linda; and John's Flies. Green, black/silver, and chartreuse are among the most consistently productive colors.

For attractors, which are tied 16-20 inches ahead of a trolling fly and sway widely from side to side, use Herring Dodger flashers; King Dodgers; the Jensen Dodger; Abe and Al flashers; and Super Flashers. Since they come in a wide variety of colors and Prism Tapes, stick to all chrome, brass/chrome, chartreuse, silver prism/chrome, white, and Chrome/Blue Prism-Lite in sizes ranging from 6-10 inches.

STRATEGIES FOR THE GIANTS

Once all the lures and tackle have been assembled, plan a trolling strategy. This strategy should include being on the water very early near daybreak, since as mentioned salmon show a distinct tendency to feed early. Also, plan to use four rods on downriggers to be fished in salmon zones. That is, each downrigger weight will be pulling a salmon lure through water 52-54 degrees very near the bottom somewhere between 40-80 feet deep. Of course, second lures can be pulled behind stacked releases up higher in the water, perhaps in the thermocline where 56-60 degree water is holding brown trout.

You should also plan a good lure spread and pattern. Plugs catch many salmon when fished right behind the boat on the inside downriggers. You should try to mix sizes on the plugs and put either a J-Plug or Tiger Plug type next to a Hot Shot or Fire Plug. The outside rigger can be used to pull spoons or flashers and squids. As for the higher releases stacked above, try to pull only spoons. A double stack of spoons on one line is very effective.

The distance behind the downrigger release mechanism shouldn't be more than 30 feet for any salmon lure. Most success is regis-

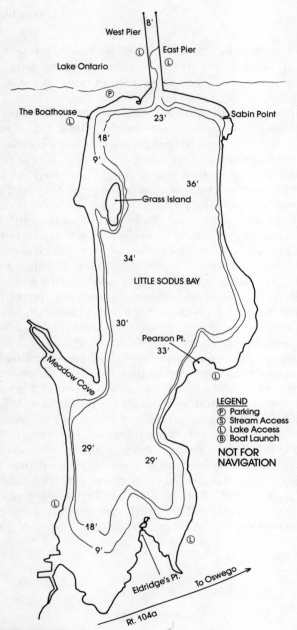

West Pier

East Pier

Lake Ontario

8'

Ⓛ

Ⓛ

Ⓟ

The Boathouse
Ⓛ

Sabin Point

23'

18'

9'

36'

Grass Island

34'

LITTLE SODUS BAY

30'

Pearson Pt.
33'

Ⓛ

Meadow Cove

LEGEND
Ⓟ Parking
Ⓢ Stream Access
Ⓛ Lake Access
Ⓑ Boat Launch

NOT FOR
NAVIGATION

29'

29'

Ⓛ

18'

9'

Ⓛ

Eldridge's Pt.

To Oswego

Rt. 104a

▶ *13b. LITTLE SODUS BAY*

tered from 15-20 feet back. However, we have taken salmon on lures fished in much closer to the weights. Since the plugs have quite an erratic pattern, always keep them in close to the boat. Spoons and squids can be trolled further back.

Boat speed is also critical. Make certain to work between 2.5-4 MPH during this late summer season. Within this already narrow range, a boat will have to find the speed most effective for its size. Since the water is relatively warm in this close for the cold blooded salmon, their metabolism rate is greatly increased. This is nature's way of giving them huge amounts of energy necessary to navigate up powerful rivers to successfully spawn (even though Pacific salmon do not spawn successfully in Lake Ontario tributaries).

A final point that should be made here is that coho salmon when hooked down below 60 feet deep are very much like "kamikaze" pilots during the second World War. Once the silver salmon feels the sting of the hook, he turns and heads as fast as he can for the surface. This unfortunate occurrence only succeeds in killing the fish, which pops up on the surface and is reeled lifeless to the net.

In summary, a chinook strike is characterized by a long blazing run, a brown or landlock will usually fight well and jump, a laker will pull well but come up quickly behind the boat remaining in the water, a steelhead will jump all over the place before settling down to fight, and a coho will leave you thinking you have nothing at all on the end of your rod as he heads for the surface. Whenever you encounter a coho strike, you must reel as fast as possible and try to overtake the fish. This is often impossible, though.

As for this giant salmon fishing, it is the most exciting in the lake. As many who have tried it would agree, it may also be the most exciting freshwater fishing in the world. The chinook fight for up to an hour and a half, and with a thirty or forty pounder on, it definitely "ain't over till it's over!" Nonetheless, for those who do not like trolling, Ch. 14 offers alternatives.

OTHER
METHODS

"Lake Ontario offers something for everyone. If trolling is not your thing, you can anchor or drift around lazily and still catch fish of wall-mount proportions."

14

Up to this point, we have dealt primarily with trolling and bait-fishing for trout and salmon, and with catching pike, bass, and pan-fish along the shoreline. In this chapter, we will discuss several new techniques for the boater. We will also talk about the Noodle Rod and introduce several controversial techniques used by anglers (where legal) in creeks, streams, and rivers.

Lake Ontario offers something for everyone. If trolling is not your thing, you can anchor or drift around lazily and still catch fish of wall mount proportions. For true "lazy man's fishing," it's tough to beat anchoring.

ANCHORING

This is a technique that offers an alternative to drifting and trolling. It comes in very handy when the wind is blowing hard (or in the wrong direction) or when there's only a small concentration of fish showing in a particular area. By drifting or trolling, you may miss the small target completely. But by anchoring, you can ignore the wind and sit all day on top of the smallest concentration of fish. Even at anchor you can cover a considerable amount of valuable territory and increase your catch if you know what you are doing.

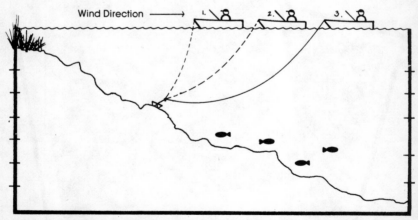

▶ *14a. FISHING AT ANCHOR — An alternative to drifting. Fish at the proper depth and temperature for the species you desire. Pay out anchor line to change locations. This is primarily a bottom fishing method. For suspended fish, drifting or trolling may be more effective.*

Using a fish finder, a thermal probe (see Ch. 8), an anchor, and about 150 feet of anchor line, try to position your boat above a good concentration of brown or lake trout. The best place to find browns during summer will be close to the bottom in 56-60 degrees of water. Look for lakers at 51 degrees right on the bottom. Set up so that your boat is blowing away from shore (if possible) on as short an anchor line as possible over the preferred temperature. The best fishing occurs when you are tethered in shallow water blowing out over deeper water with the lower limit of the preferred temperature zone just touching the bottom.

To set up this scenario, ride offshore and take several water temperature readings at different depths until you have found either the 60 degree or the 51 degree temperature zone. Make note of the depth and extent of the zone. Since brown and lake trout hug the bottom, ride in towards the shoreline until you are in the depth at which you have discovered the correct temperature for the species you intend to fish. Recheck the bottom temperature. It should be close to the temperature you want. At this time, you can adjust your position accordingly. If the temperature is too high, go offshore some. If it is too low, go inshore. Once in perfect position, keep an eye on your fish finder unit and ride parallel to the shoreline (along lines of equal contour) looking for fish in the zone near the bottom. When you make contact, check the wind direction and anchor so that the wind will blow your boat over the located fish.

Now you're ready to get your bait into the water. You can hook minnows or sawbellies (alewife herring) under the dorsal fin making sure to bring the barb forward. Or you can sew the bait on in such a way that if a fish bites, it is almost certain of being hooked. The accompanying drawings, Fig. 14-b, show exactly how to do this.

Correctly executed, only the two barbs should be showing, and both will be in position so that when a gamefish takes the baitfish head on (as they usually do), it will not be able to spit the bait out without getting hooked. When you get a strike using this rig, you almost always hook a fish.!

I can remember thinking, when I first used this rig, that the fragile herring would never survive the needle and would quickly die. However, this wasn't the case, and now I rig for all species this way.

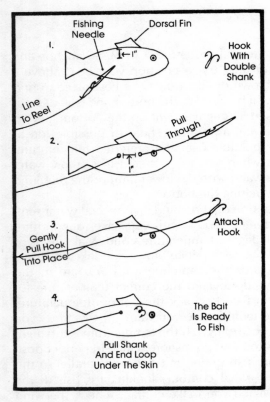

1. Fishing Needle · Dorsal Fin · I←1"

Line To Reel

Hook With Double Shank

2. Pull Through · I" 1"

3. Gently Pull Hook Into Place · Attach Hook

4. The Bait Is Ready To Fish

Pull Shank And End Loop Under The Skin

14b.
SEWING A SAWBELLY

Using a trout rig (see Fig.14-c), drop your bait to the bottom and reel up several cranks to get your baitfish swimming freely above the bottom. To make certain that it is, place your outfit in a rod holder and watch the tip of your rod. If the bait is swimming freely, the tip will be moving. If it is not moving, raise the bait up another crank. Once you're satisfied that everything is in order, open your bail and place your line in a Strike Guard. A Strike Guard is a device that keeps your line from coming off an open-bailed spinning reel. Once the fish strikes, the line snaps out of the Strike Guard's ball bearing with an audible "click" signaling the strike. The fish is then allowed to swim off with the bait unaware that he is also towing along some line. Set two rods up in this manner if fishing alone, or three if you are fishing with someone else (the law reads only two rods per angler).

This technique clicks well with brown and lake trout which spend a good part of their time hugging the bottom while searching for food in their preferred temperature zones. They both show a preference for live minnows and herring suspended about a foot above the bottom. When a trout is interested in your bait, you'll know it! Your rod will begin bouncing all around. When the trout grabs your bait, the tip of your rod will dive for the water and the Strike Guard will sound. Line will begin coming freely off your spool. At this point, you should pick up the rod, engage the reel, crank up any slack line and upon feeling the fish, strike immediately.

After catching a few fish (or especially if you're not catching any) consider paying out more anchor line. This will enable you to cover additional territory. By moving slightly in this fashion, you may move into bigger fish, or even into more action. Should the action or size of the fish decrease, you can always go back to your first location by simply retrieving some line. Should the fish not cooperate anywhere along your anchor line, find another patch of fish and begin the process again.

DRIFTING

This is a technique whereby live bait is fished under a boat that is being moved along by either wind or current. The technique is often used to catch brown trout that have moved off the bottom (perhaps while chasing bait or in search of more oxygenated water) and are suspended 10-30 feet deep in their preferred temperature zone. In this situation, it matters not how deep the water is.

Along with smelt, landlocked herring or "saw-belly" is Ontario's premier baitfish.

Using one of the three rigs shown in Fig. 14-c, place a lively baitfish under enough weight (½ to 1 ounce), and lower it into the proper temperature zone. The sinker will keep the bait down, while the 3-foot leader will allow it plenty of room to swim around. When a gamefish approaches, the baitfish will swim frantically for its life. This nervous reaction usually prompts a savage strike from the gamefish.

When using herring, it is recommended that you fish only three bait per 16-foot or smaller boat. The baits should be positioned (see Fig. 14-d) so that the swimming baitfish can't get together and tangle the lines. Fish one rod off the bow, one amidships and the third off the stern. To effectively spread the bait through the preferred temperature zone, keep the rod nearest the drift highest in the water and the one midships the deepest as shown in Fig. 14-e.

Once a fish takes the bait and your line snaps out of a Strike Guard, engage the reel, point the rod at the running fish, allow it to take up the slack line, and then reach back on the rod and set the hook. Some anglers give the fish time to swallow the bait, but this isn't necessary. Once the big fish has the bait in his mouth, he will swim off and you can strike immediately.

Of course, I have experimented with just how long to wait before

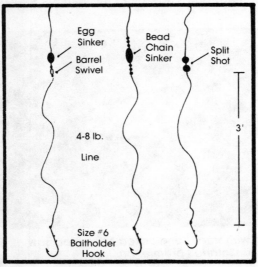

Egg Sinker

Bead Chain Sinker

Split Shot

Barrel Swivel

4-8 lb.

Line

3'

Size #6 Baitholder Hook

14c.
LIVE BAIT DRIFT RIGS
The bait will be able to swim three feet in any direction from the weight.

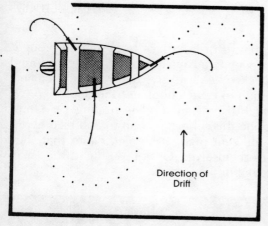

Direction of Drift

striking. On occasion, I have counted up to 30 seconds or longer before striking. However, even after such a long wait, the fish can be missed. When striking immediately, I have found that more fish are hooked.

The best bait are from 3-5 inches long. They should also be very lively. Baitfishermen: Don't overlook the nighttime potential of this lake! Big brown trout feed well at night, so fish for them anytime around the clock.

For lake trout during the day, use the same rigs. But instead of fishing in 56-60 degrees of water as you would for browns, lower your bait to where the 51 degree zone meets bottom, preferably just above some structure. You can simply do this by dropping the bait all the way to the bottom and reeling up several cranks. Set the rod in position, and wait for the Strike Guard to signal.

Often before a gamefish actually strikes, the rod's tip will go crazy jumping up and down as the little baitfish battles for its life by nervously running all around. This sign of impending action should alert the anxious angler to get ready.

NIGHT FISHING

To fish the witching hours, you can troll, drift, or anchor. While drifting or at anchor, do everything the same as above, except have a strong Halogen lantern or light beaming into the water. The light will attract baitfish and the trout will set up under them. A classic scene is seeing baitfish on a recorder down the first 10-15 feet and giant blips another 5-7 feet below them (so try to position your bait just below the attracted baitfish). Even lake trout can be brought up from their preferred temperature zone to feed on stragglers found swimming beneath the pack. Of course, give them all the stragglers they want, just make certain to have a hook in each one.

Another productive nightfishing method is trolling for kings. Although I have never done this, I have spoken to and read about many who have. These diligent night fishermen claim that they have the lake virtually to themselves. On a busy night, they may encounter only a half dozen or fewer boats.

One picture is worth a thousand words. Here, bait is suspended 17 feet under our night lights. Below them are big
lakers and browns.

The best time of year for night trolling seems to be during late summer, from mid-August on, when the salmon group up in front of their spawning rivers. This is shallow trolling, usually from the shoreline out to about 40 feet of water. Calm nights with little wind are most inviting; make certain, though, to bring along a compass

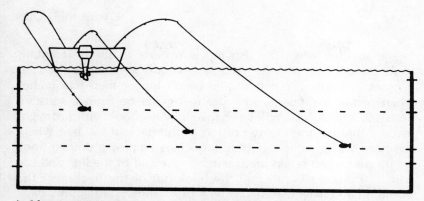

▶14e. DRIFTING LIVE BAIT — The deeper baits should be off the middle backside of the drift. This will cut down on tangles. Once a fish is hooked, someone should reel in the other baits immediately.

or other navigational device just in case fog or some other adverse weather sets in.

Begin trolling near an inlet (salmon usually enter the inlets late in the afternoon or at night) using rattling "glo in the dark" and "chemically illuminated" lures. Examples are the Dandy-Glo, Hot N' Tot, Pearl Poptail, Jensen's Fishback, Kingfisher spoon, Luhr Jensen's Super Duper, and the #5 rattling J-Plug. Try to troll in water showing 54-56 degrees whenever possible and keep your lures in the upper 5-10 feet of water. Troll fast, somewhere between 3½-5 MPH using flat lines or downriggers.

Kings feed well at night, and fish that have been lethargic and laying around on the bottom all day long generally become very active two to three hours after dusk. They usually school up and chase baitfish until midnight. Then, they seem to rest for a while, only to become active again between 4 AM and dawn. These fish will chase and strike lures. One important thing to remember is this: If you can recognize that you are into a school of fish, try not to troll down the middle of them. By picking away on the out-skirts of the school, more salmon will be fought and caught.

One last word has to do with safety. Make certain to equip your boat with law-required flare kits, floatation devices and proper light-ing (bow and stern running lights). It wouldn't hurt to tell someone back at the dock approximately where you're planning to fish.

MOOCHING
Mooching is another method used to catch trout and salmon late

in the summer when the fish move in close to shore. It entails using a dead bait with its head and entrails removed and cut to a point in front. The bait should be no longer than five inches when prepared properly. In order to rig the bait run a Mustad-Sproat 2/0 hook, or any long-shanked, heavy hook with a straight eye, up through the meaty portion of the back of the bait where the head was attached. (Often, moochers employ a double hook set-up where two hooks are snelled on the end of the line and the bait is strung on both.) Pull the hook out of the back near the dorsal fin and twist it around. Run it down through the upper back so that the shaft runs along the back while the barb is pointed forward and lays alongside or under the bait. Pull the line taut and with enough weight 24-30 inches ahead of the bait, drop it down to the bottom.

For tackle, try to use medium action 8½ foot spinning rods and reels. The whole secret in mooching is to allow the rod to dip and dive as it pulls the weight and bait through the water. If the bait jumps off the bottom and darts all around, game fish become very interested and attack. The more flexible medium action spinning rod has just enough spring to pull off this deception.

With your baited rods (up to four well spread) placed in rod holders, engage your engine and pull the baits up 30-50 feet off the bottom. Now, cut the engine and allow the baits to settle back down toward the bottom. Mix this process with trolling the baits along slowly enough to have them flutter or spin several feet off the bottom. Continue both of these procedures until you get a strike. Mooching works best during the day and in from 60-80 feet of water.

If there's a strong wind blowing, you can also drift and allow your baits to bounce along the bottom. These motions may be interpreted by salmon as baitfish scurrying for cover. By using real baitfish, the smells will be right and if the action is enticing enough, it may cause a resting salmon to chase and strike.

In either case (mooching or drifting), make certain to adjust the drags on your reels so that they will be able to stand up to the bottom bouncing or forward thrust of the engine and still give off line properly should a salmon strike. With the drag screaming, tighten down some and strike the fleeting fish.

NOODLE RODS

Noodle Rods are long and slender steelhead rods used to fish very light line. They run from 9-14 feet in length, with many popular models such as the Loomis Composite Noodle Sticks being 11½ feet long. The weight of this rod will range from 3½ ounces up to 5½. Although most models suggest using 4 lb. test line, the great flexibility of the rods will even allow you to go down to 2 lb. test leaders. I'm not saying 2 lb. test is practical, just possible.

With noodle rods, anglers can effectively fish deep pools that are very near to them by dropping their bait through the pool, rather than by casting into it. This is very important when steelheading with very light line, because when casting, rigs tend to get stuck on the bottom. By simply dropping, your rod holds the weight above the bottom and your rig rarely gets stuck.

The best part about noodle rods is that once a fish is hooked, the rod will take the brunt of the action. Every quick move the fish makes will be absorbed by the length of the rod, and so you'll have a greater chance of landing a fish than with a short, conventional rod.

SNATCHING AND LIFTING

These are techniques used by anglers where legal in specially designated rivers or sections of rivers (see Ch. 17). Some feel these methods aren't really fishing at all, and they do turn a lot of people off. Yet they permit greater utilization of the salmon resource.

Snatching and lifting are really hooking actions whereby an unsuspecting salmon is hooked with a weighted treble anywhere in its body (snatching) or with a single hook in its open mouth (lifting). The reason these techniques are permitted is twofold. First, the vast majority of Pacific coast salmon (chinook and coho) entering the rivers and streams to spawn have no interest at all in feeding. Second, if these techniques were not allowed, it is argued that the vast majority of salmon, which die after spawning anyway, would simply rot along the stream.

What's ironic about the situation is that most anglers think snatching and lifting are easy. Yet I have spent many hours watching the method in operation, and know that a large number of anglers trying to snag salmon actually go fishless.

To be successful, you must be a good hunter. The key is to hunt the fish and then set about to catch him. Once you see a target (using polaroid glasses) you direct your weighted treble hook just beyond it and pull. If the fish gets hooked, hang on! He'll usually come flying up and out of the water instantly. Then, he'll head off for parts unknown. If your drag isn't working, your line will get extremely taut and either break, or the weighted treble will pull free and come flying back at you at a very dangerous speed. Considering the number of people in most snagging sections, it is quite amazing that more do not get hurt.

With lifting, you try to find a salmon that is resting alongside some underwater obstacle like a boulder, or splashing through rapids between pools. Once the fish has been observed, try to position yourself above it and attempt to run your bait or line into its open mouth. The moment either enters its mouth, "lift" your rod and try to pull your hook into its bony jaw. Unfortunately, many anglers get frustrated with uncooperative salmon in the non-snagging, non-lifting stretches and revert to this process. Since the hook winds up in the fish's mouth, who's to say that the fish didn't bite? Be warned that this technique is strictly illegal outside the snagging zones, and game wardens do watch for and arrest fishermen who lift where it's not allowed.

Anglers in some snatching sections practice the less sportsman-like, but legal, approach of blind snatching. In this approach, they can't see the fish because the water is too deep or dark. They just cast out and allow their hooks to settle to the bottom. Then, they pull the hooks as hard as possible and if there's a salmon between them, sometimes they connect. But, most times they don't!

Several years back, while talking with some hatchery personnel at the Suffern Outdoor Exposition in New York, I was told that during the snagging season (August 15-October 15 on the Salmon River) very few adult salmon actually make it back to the hatchery, which is above the snagging section. Yet, once the season ends, the hatchery gets all the fish needed for its operations. This proves that lifting and snagging work, and that these methods provide many anglers with the opportunity to hook and catch salmon that would otherwise simply die and rot along the bank. No matter what your personal view, these methods are part of the careful management of the Lake Ontario resource, and they have been implemented by biologists who know a lot more about the subject than you or I.

ICE
FISHING

"Ontario ice fishing has one difference. When a flag pops, it might be a perch. But it also might be something as big as your kid."

▼

15

For many anglers, the slamming of winter's icy door marks the end of another fishing season. For others, though, it's only the start of their favorite season. Beginning on November 15th or soon after when there's sufficient ice to cover the backwaters (the main lake never freezes), the cold but productive ice fishing season gets under way. With fish caught from Wilson Harbor in the west right around to the Thousand Islands, area residents don't have too far to travel to get in on the action. The season runs until April 15 with good to excellent catches made all along the coast everywhere there's safe ice conditions.

As the cold weather moves in, northern counties like Oswego, Jefferson, and St. Lawrence get the first ice. Hence, ice fishing kicks off in the northeast corner of the lake first. Often, it's this initial week of the ice fishing season that offers the greatest potential. The water is still relatively warm (for winter) with surface temperatures showing 32 degrees. Down only a few feet, the water will be 39.4 degrees or so. With this warmer water underneath, fish remain pretty active for the first couple of weeks. Then, as the water loses any remaining warmth, and oxygen levels fall, fishing becomes more difficult with fish feeding less and only during certain periods.

SAFETY FIRST
If the ice offers the most potential during this period, it also poses the most danger. Ice that may be thick enough to stand on may not support the active pursuit of fish. Here are some guidelines for ice thickness safety that you would be well advised to know and follow: Two inches thick will support one person walking; four inches — one person fishing; five inches — snowmobile; and 8-12 inches — car or light truck. Keep in mind that new ice is stronger than old ice which may have thawed and been refrozen several times. Also keep in mind that there can always be weak spots, especially where there are strong currents or where streams enter. Extreme caution at all times is urged.

In the bays and ponds that freeze solid, from 9-15 inches of ice can be expected. Hand augers are sufficient to get the job done, but gas augers will do the work faster and with less wear and tear on your body.

Ontario ice fishing has one difference. When a flag pops it might be a perch. But it also might be something as big as your kid.

Northern pike, bass, and perch are very active and feed well while attempting to put on one last layer of body fat to help them through the impending winter. Trout (steelhead and brown) may also be caught as they try to enter some creeks from under the ice. These are considered bonus fish by many unsuspecting, lucky anglers.

Once while fishing out of the Wigwam Hotel, which is the main access to North Pond, our party caught close to 100 perch while jigging grubs on light Swedish Pimples. We also caught three northerns, the largest of which went eight pounds, on blue streaked Kastmasters. We fished in water which was about 10 feet deep out approximately 300 yards directly in front of the hotel restaurant. There were so many anglers out there, over 100, that it looked like a miniature city! Some were skating and fishing, but most were just fishing. By the way, the sweet-eating yellow is appreciated up this way, and back at the Wigwam perch were being purchased from successful ice anglers for $0.80 cents a pound.

As the season progresses, the warmer water (39 degrees) gets deeper in the lake, and water in bays and coves becomes the same relative cold temperature throughout. Once this occurs, fish begin feeding in certain patterns. For example, fish feed especially well when a warm front or low pressure area is approaching. The front is often accompanied by freezing rain or snow; however, when it begins to precipitate, the flags begin to fly. If you are aware of a warm front's approach, plan to be out on the ice.

Be prepared for the cold. The entire region is subject to sub-zero temperatures all winter long. Also, since Lake Ontario never entirely freezes — only the bays and ponds and the lake for maybe a short distance out — you can expect moist air to be coming in off the lake all winter long. Moist air usually mixes with cold air to form snow and snow it does. So, be prepared. Also, if you get the chance, try to view the big lake. Ice flows often pile up in magnificent displays along the beach. This is especially true after a strong blow out of the northeast.

A FEW STRATEGIES

On weekdays, you can plan to get on the ice around 9 AM. With some prior planning you should have some idea where to set up camp. With the aid of a map and some advice from local anglers and tackle shops, try to pick a location where the water is from

4-10 feet deep and where the fish have easy access to deeper water. Although many fish settle down deep in the lake (that's where the warmer water is during the winter), they usually migrate up into 4-10 feet of water to feed.

Set up your tip-ups in a pattern. For the best results, set them in a straight line about 30 feet apart. The reason for this is, once the ice gets crowded with anglers, you will be better able to keep track of which tip-ups are yours. If you position yourself at one end, you will be able to see everything that's happening to all your tip-ups at a single glance.

Run your string of tip-ups either from deeper water into shallower water, or along a common depth (say six feet). If you aren't getting any action whatsoever, move your holes 30 feet to the right or left. By doing so, you will at least maintain the same relative depth at each position and have only minimum adjustments to each rig. Of course if nothing pops, you may have to change depths or locations considerably.

WHERE TO ICE FISH
There are many spots where excellent, early season fishing can be had. Along the St. Lawrence you have fine northern pike locations at Wellesley Island State Park, Grasse Point State Park, around Clayton, and Burnham Point State Park. Moving into Lake Ontario, fish Three Mile Bay, Chaumont Bay, Sackets Harbor, Henderson's Harbor, South Sandy Creek by Lakeview Marsh, and the North and South Ponds.

Some good locations to try during the week that are very crowded on weekends include: Twelve Mile Creek near Wilson for northerns, perch and trout; Braddocks Bay for northern pike, yellow perch, panfish, brown trout and rainbow trout; Sodus Bay near Eagle Island and off Thorton Point by 2nd Creek for northerns and perch; Port Bay (an excellent location) for northerns, perch, and panfish; Little Sodus Bay for northerns, perch, trout, and an occasional pickerel; and North and South Ponds above the Salmon River for perch with an occasional northern mixed in.

On weekends plan to be on the ice early, not because you will necessarily catch more fish, but because you can then be certain of getting your favorite spot. There will be many more anglers out. Definitely set up a straight line pattern on weekends.

To try and beat the weekend crowds, you might fish at: Oak Orchard Creek for northerns, perch, and trout; Waterport Pond (Lake Alice) a northern hotspot where Otter Creek enters; Buck Pond and Irondequoit Bay near Rochester for northern pike, perch, brown and rainbow trout; the Pond in Fair Haven State Park for northerns; Oswego Harbor for perch, trout, and panfish; the Little Salmon River for northerns and perch; and anywhere throughout the Henderson-Chaumont area where fishing can be good to excellent and where there's so much room you can't get crowded.

Let's look at a typical ice fishing day. No need to rise exceptionally early. Let the air warm up a bit before venturing out onto the ice. Make certain to check all your gear before leaving home base. You should be certain to have with you:

1. A large wooden box to haul the majority of gear
2. 5 tip-ups, with your name and address clearly marked (the law)

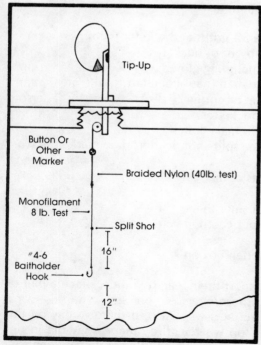

15a.
TYPICAL ICE FISHING RIG

Keep your bait one foot above bottom or above the top of any weeds. Use the button to indicate proper depth. Then, whenever replacing bait, the button will allow you to get the bait back to the original position.

3. 2 hand held lines (jigging rods)
4. Lure case
5. Bait containers — one for grubs and one for minnows
6. Net for getting baitfish out of bucket
7. Thermal everything, including gloves
8. Perhaps a topographic map (nautical chart) of the area
9. Thermos with hot soup or coffee
10. A grill (either gas or brickettes)
11. Lunch or ingredients to make lunch
12. Terminal tackle: hooks, split-shot, leaders, line markers & depth sounders
13. Spud bar or auger (gas or manual)
14. Skimmer
15. Ice cleats (needed on smooth ice only)
16. Several buckets for your catch
17. A gaff
18. A sled to put the wooden box on

Many use sleds to transport their gear. If you do, place a pair of children's toy skis under the runners of your sled. The skis won't stick to the ice like the runners will. Also, if there's snow on the ice, the skis will stay on top whereas the runners may dig in unevenly causing problems like dumping the sled and its contents.

A FEW MORE STRATEGIES

You can also set up your tip-ups with 40-80 pound test braided nylon line (the heavier line is preferred), and a six foot leader made out of 8-12 pound test monofilament. Place a regular shirt button with the line running through two holes up on the braided nylon line. Tie a barrel swivel to the 80 pound test line, and add the leader to the other end. Then, attach a size #4-10 baitholder hook (size #4 for northerns, sizes #6-10 for panfish) to the end of the line and place a split-shot about 14 inches above the hook. Now all five tip-ups will be set up and it's much easier to do this inside than out in the frigid elements. I would further recommend that you consult local tackle shops about tackle and gear for a particular area you may want to fish.

Also, each county around the lake maintains an area hotline to keep anglers abreast of the fishing conditions and catches being made locally. See Fig. 5-c in Chapter 5.

Upon arriving at the spot you want to fish, there are certain things you can do to maximize your potential. First find out how deep the water is. You can do this by using a line with a heavy weight on it. Lower the weight until it strikes the bottom. Now, get a good hold on the line at water level and back up until the weight is on the ice. This length of line will indicate how deep the water is. Some makers of depth recorders now make units that see very well through the ice; with some all you need is wet ice or a small puddle on which to place the transducer.

▶ *Perch and pike are the more common ice fishing staples. but trout and even steelhead can spice things up.*

Stretch out your tip-ups alongside the depth line. Make certain to set your line so that it is about 18 inches off bottom and place the button by the spool so that every time you use this tip-up, you will be able to return it to the button or the exact same depth. Now hook a minnow under the anterior dorsal fin and lower it into the water. If looking for pike, use an eight inch wire leader between line and hook. For all other species, no leader is required. If the bait gets down into weeds, the line entering the water will point straight down and not move. If this happens, you should move the button down 12 inches closer to the bait, reel up that far, and try again. Eventually, the bait will be suspended freely with the line moving around.

It may seem obvious, but you can lay flat on the ice and look into the hole you have made. By covering your head and the hole with a blanket or jacket, you will be able to see the bottom and any weeds that may be present. You may even see fish! Remember, you often will want your bait about one foot above the bottom or above the weeds.

Using a hand held rod with bait is often fun. You can suspend grubs, wax worms, garden worms, pieces of fish, mousie grubs, or mealworms on a hook beneath a float which sits on the water with your bait down to the desired depth. Now, the deeper you get, the more you must employ a slip bobber. That is, you pull the line through the bobber until you've reached the required depth. Then you twist the bobber until it just holds the line. Once a strike is registered, you hook and reel in the fish. When the bobber reaches the end of your rod, line goes through it.

It pays to carry a good assortment of ice jigs — both styles and sizes. Shown (left to right) are Kastmaster Blue Streak, Swedish Pimple, smaller Swedish Pimple, dot jig, Kastmaster and Jigging Rapala.

JIGS CAN BE KILLERS

Ice jigs used on jigging poles can be extremely effective. For catching sunfish, the Tear-dot, Speck, Panti Ant, and Spider Jig are productive. Fish the jig alone, or add a grub or piece of worm. For yellow and white perch, use a Diamond Back, Jig-A-Spoon, Rapala Jigging Lure, Swedish Pimple, small blue-streaked Kastmaster, or a Panfish Jig. You can adorn these jigs with worms, small minnows, or grubs. For northerns and pickerel use large blue-streaked Kastmasters, ¼-½ ounce red and white spoons, Swedish Pimples, Rapala Jigging Lures, Tinsel Tail Bucktails, and Johnson's Weedless Spoon with or without small pieces of minnow attached.

Jigging is simple. Just drop your jig down to the bottom, reel up one foot and begin making short jerks with the rod's tip. The jig will bounce around and eventually get some attention. When a good fish takes hold, you will not be able to raise the rod's tip. In that event lift extra hard and set the hook. Should the fish make a run in any direction other than up, consider putting your rod's tip into the hole and under the ice. This will save your line from rubbing dangerously against the sharp edge of the hole.

EXCITEMENT ON THE TRIBUTARIES

PART III

THE ALTMAR HATCHERY

"Every year, Altmar raises about 3 million trout and salmon for release into Lake Ontario. Growth rates are phenomenal, with salmon reaching 30 pounds in about 4 years."

16

Located above the quaint little village of Altmar, the *Salmon River Trout & Salmon Hatchery* (often called Altmar) sits astride Beaverdam Brook which flows directly into the Salmon River just upstream from the Altmar Bridge. One of the major suppliers of fish to both Lake Ontario and Lake Erie, the hatchery's operations consist of hatching eggs, growing fish, catching fish returning to spawn, and stripping eggs from female fish while fertilizing them with the milt of male fish to start the hatching process all over again. Fish raised here include brown and rainbow trout, coho and chinook salmon and some new fish which we'll discuss.

DEC PROGRAMS

Before we talk about the specific operation of the unique Altmar hatchery, it would be valuable to cover current stocking policies concerning Lake Ontario. Before the stocking program, lake trout that had once been plentiful were all but eliminated. Now, the DEC is trying to get this species back on its feet. With an intensive lamprey control program, reduced take limits and a dedicated federal lake trout restocking program, it is hoped that the once naturally reproducing fish will become self-sustaining again. There is already documentation of some successful lake trout spawning over the past few seasons.

As mentioned in Ch. 2, Lake Ontario once had an extraordinary population of landlocked salmon (Atlantic salmon that had become cut off from the sea in a past geologic time). Like the lake trout, this species was nearly wiped out in Lake Ontario, but now a restoration program is underway. Unlike lake trout, which spawn on offshore shoals, the landlocks return to the stream of their birth (or where they were stocked). Since the DEC only stocks three streams with these salmon, they can keep a close eye on the program and measure its effectiveness. For one thing, they shut the streams to fishing during the spawning period. This enables the species to reproduce and the DEC biologists to evaluate the numbers of returning fish. The long range goal of the department is to see a naturally sustaining population of landlocked salmon in the big lake once again.

Other fish are stocked annually, but without the hope of their becoming natural populations. The Pacific salmon, for example, will always be hatchery reared. The same holds true for the brown and rainbow trout, although some natural reproduction of these trout does take place. As for some of the warm water species — bass, muskellunge, and certain panfish — they're reared in hatcheries and used to supplement the lake's naturally occurring populations.

Not only does the DEC attempt to revitalize and maintain species, but they also conduct extensive experiments with new and exciting species (see later in this Chapter). With all the time, money, and effort going into studying, rearing and releasing these gamefish, new success stories are bound to be written on Lake Ontario and its tributaries.

HATCHERY OPERATIONS

The Altmar hatchery, as mentioned, is located on Beaverdam Brook, which is a small, short tributary of the Salmon River. The hatchery has a pretty nifty operation. It releases small fish it has hatched into its own holding pond. From the pond the fish run through an outlet shoot into the brook. From there, it's downstream to the salmon river and 13 miles out to Lake Ontario. Once in the lake, they remain for several years. They feed voraciously with some attaining weights in excess of 45 pounds. Upon reaching sexual maturity, they turn around and swim right back to the hatchery. Of course on their return trip, they're greeted by many smiling anglers lining the entire stretch of the Salmon River.

The operation of any hatchery is a year round job. Beginning in September, Altmar personnel begin preparing for the returning adult salmon (coho and chinook). The adult salmon swim up from Lake Ontario normally from mid-September through November depending upon water flow and temperature and make their way up the fish ladder.

Come November, the spawn house starts slowing down. There are still some salmon in the brook and ladder, but visitor numbers decrease. With some five million chinook and three million coho salmon eggs collected, the incubation process begins. The hatchery closes to the public November 30th then reopens again March 15th.

During the time the hatchery is closed to the public, coho and chinook eggs begin to hatch. Personnel rid the incubators of dead eggs, and the salmon sac-fry (a stage where the fish is fed from its own yolk sac) are moved into tanks inside the building. In a normal year, three to four million chinook fry and one million coho fry will be hatched.

Also at this time, fall-run steelhead start swimming up from the

lake. Some move into the fish ladder and are held in ponds for egg take later in the spring.

During January and February chinook and coho fry grow until they are two inches long. Also at this time, experimental egg takes of between 100,000 to 200,000 are made from steelhead which have been brought into the warm building to ripen early.

When March 15th rolls around, Altmar reopens its doors. The public gets treated to the spawn house steelhead egg collection operation where over two million eggs are taken. Adult fish (spawnouts from 10-20 pounds) are returned alive back to the river in hatchery trucks. Chinook and cohos are two-three inches long. It is a good time for public viewing.

The steelhead egg collection is completed in April and the vigorous stocking schedule starts. The hatchery fish are now all 12-14 months old (last year's eggs) with the brown trout averaging 8-10 inches, domestic rainbows 7-10 inches, steelhead 5-8 inches, and coho salmon 5-8 inches long. Tributaries entering Lake Erie and Lake Ontario are stocked daily during this period by hatchery fish transportation vehicles.

Brown trout and domestic rainbows are released offshore. Since they aren't considered a migratory species, the department feels it senseless to put them into a stream, especially when they may just remain there. To preclude this possibility, they're stocked offshore and only later will they enter streams to spawn or to follow the big salmon (which the trout shadow looking to feast upon salmon eggs).

CHEMICAL IMPRINTING

The cohos are released in early April, browns in mid-April, rainbows in late-April, and the chinook in early May. The important part of successful salmonoid rearing is to make sure that smoltification (parr-smolt transformation) occurs in the river in which you want the fish to return. Smoltification is the process whereby the salmon imprint certain water characteristics into memory so that years later, when they are mature and ready to spawn, they will be able to return to the area in which they were released.

Each species undergoes smoltification at a different time in its development. Once smoltified, they are ready to run downstream and out into either the ocean, or in this case, the lake. If they hatched naturally in some wild river, chinook would smoltify in 5-6 months, while cohos, browns, and steelhead would remain in the river until they were 13-14 months old. Life in the wild is very dangerous for the young of the species, but hatchery rearing avoids most of the calamities and the young fish have a much better chance for survival.

As May arrives, steelhead hatch and salmon continue moving outside into the raceways. Chinook fry are now three inches long and are stocked in tributaries to both Lake Erie and Lake Ontario. At this point, the release of 800,000 chinook fry into the Salmon River has been completed. The chinook fry leave the hatchery as three to five inch long, five to six month old fish.

June and July are very slow months at the hatchery. Personnel feed the juvenile fish and constantly clean the raceways. Visitors can view a slide show and walk around the grounds.

In August, the water temperature is in the 60s and the following inventories are usually on hand:

Species	Usual Inventory	Size
Brown trout	200,000-400,000	5-7'' (10-20 per lb.)
Rainbow trout	50,000-100,000	5-8'' (10-20 per lb.)
Coho Salmon	500,000	5-7'' (10-20 per lb.)
Steelhead	500,000	4-5'' (30-50 per lb.)

In September, the entire procedure starts all over again.

From this description, you can see that there's much to be done at the hatchery. Demanding schedules and constant attention must be paid to every aspect of the entire program if it's to be successful.

EXCITING NEW POSSIBILITIES

Other fish being experimented with for possible introduction to Lake Ontario (not all necessarily at Altmar) include Skamania Steelhead, landlocked salmon, Atlantic salmon and Bavarian Seeforellen (brown trout).

The Skamania, which have been acquired from the State of Michigan, have been earmarked for release into Stony Creek, Catfish Creek, the Oswego River, Maxwell Creek, and the Niagara River. With the first batch of fish already stocked, biologists expected the first run of these fast growing rainbows to occur in August of '87. However, this first run would have been only mature two year old fish, so the years following this initial run should get better.

The Skamania steelhead are known to remain in very close to shore all summer long. There, trollers should be able to catch them in the upper 25 feet or so of water by long lining spoons and swimming plugs, very much in the manner of "ice-out" fishing. This new inshore fishery should be very popular and exciting.

Stocking programs for landlocked salmon and Atlantic salmon — the latter new to the lake — have begun. The landlocks have been stocked in several creeks located around the state. They are presently in Irondequoit Creek, Lindsey Creek and the Little Sandy Creek while Penobscot Atlantic salmon (purely experimental) are being released in Little Sandy Creek and Lindsey Creek. Remember, these three creeks are off limits to fishermen from October 1 to November 30th when hatchery personnel maintain a watch for mature Atlantics returning to spawn.

This past year, landlocked salmon were caught weighing up to 15 pounds. Next year, these very same fish should go close to 20. With the addition of Atlantic salmon, look out! These fish grow to 40 pounds or better, and unlike the chinook salmon which spawn and die, Atlantics return year after year to spawn.

The Bavarian Seeforellen program is also underway with DEC having gotten 45,000 of these select fish from a West German hatchery. The first shipment of eggs was received last year and the hatched fry were placed in some experimental NYS waters. If the species shows that it can survive, it will be added to the list of big fish presently roaming Lake Ontario.

Besides Altmar, there are other hatcheries stocking trout and salmon into Lake Ontario. The Rome Lab hatchery releases thousands of steelhead trout fingerlings (about 130 per pound), brown

A SPORT FISHERY IS BORN

1968 25,000 COHO SALMON FROM THE STATE OF MICHIGAN WERE STOCKED IN THE SPRING BROOK RESERVOIR PULASKI, NEW YORK

SINCE 1968 NEW YORK STATE HAS STOCKED MORE THAN **9000000** SALMON IN THE GREAT LAKES

NEW CHALLENGE OR NEW YORK'S ANGLERS

BUILDING A FISHERY IT ALL ADDS UP

AN EFFECTIVE STOCKING POLICY

PARASITE CONTROL PROGRAM

LAMPREY CONTROL

POLLUTION ABATEMENT

GREAT LAKES THE LARGEST FRESH WATER RESERVOIR IN THE WORLD

RESEARCH

ABUNDANT FOOD SUPPLY

ALEWIFE

Wall charts, a slide show and other hatchery activities are waiting to greet visitors to the fascinating Altmar hatchery.

trout and Skamania steelhead. The Adirondack and Cortland hatcheries grow landlocked salmon for release, while all the lake trout stocked in Lake Ontario come from the Alleghany Federal hatchery in Pennsylvania.

The DEC also monitors fish development, deployment, and diets around the big lake through fish catch and belly surveys (usually conducted during cash prize tournaments and or at the mouths of many inlets). Department biologists collect biomass data necessary to construct ecological portraits for better managment.

PROFILES
OF THE MAIN
TRIBUTARIES

*"The Niagara River is awesome,
and the Salmon River is
phenomenal. But if you seek
solitude you can find it on the
lesser-known tributaries."*

17

Although much has been written about the fabled Salmon River, which runs through the Village of Pulaski and empties into Lake Ontario along its eastern shore, there are many other large tributaries to the great lake. Here, in addition to discussing the Salmon River in detail, we will profile these large but lesser-known rivers: The mighty Niagara, 18 Mile Creek, the Genesee River, Irondequoit Creek, and the Oswego River. Besides describing these waters, we will make a few historical references as to what some of them were like in a previous time.

THE NIAGARA RIVER
More like a giant extension of the lake itself, the lower Niagara River (below the magnificent Niagara Falls) is the lower link in the connection between Lakes Erie and Ontario. From the falls to Lake Ontario is a distance of just over six miles. As deep as 160 feet in places, the river gets as wide as two football fields as it travels at speeds of over 20 MPH from south to north between spectacular 300 foot cliffs. Though swift and wide, it presents much opportunity to anglers on a wide variety of great gamefish.

In this year round fishing spot anglers can try for smallmouth bass, yellow perch, trout (lake, rainbow and brown), walleye, carp, catfish, smelt, coho and giant chinook salmon. Drifting, trolling, and still fishing all have their place here, and these methods are discussed in the next chapter.

For boat fishermen the lower Niagara offers many protected bays. Nonetheless, because of currents one can still count on moving at a good clip along the shoreline through various drifts (see Fig. 17-a). Fishing can be done on this protected river even when large storms are ravaging the big lake. Since the river is very much like the lake, you can employ many of the very same trolling techniques described in earlier chapters. Drifting and still fishing from anchor are also very productive.

Launch ramps exist at Fort Niagara and Lewiston. Here excellent smallmouth fishing is done all summer long. The best way to catch the bass is by trolling Hot N'Tot lures behind bright colored downrigger cannonballs or by drifting crabs or hellgrammites.

Good drifts include Devil's Hole just south of the Robert Moses Power Plant, Artpark, Johnson's, and the Coast Guard Drift running from the launch ramp in Fort Niagara straight out the inlet in tight to shore. Here, the shallow shelf waters of Lake Ontario's New York

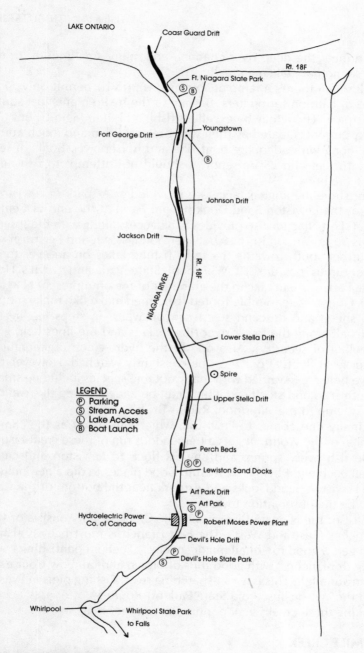

▶ 17a. THE LOWER NIAGARA RIVER

shore meet the deep river channel, and many smallmouth, trout, and salmon are taken annually.

Although there's a ramp at Youngstown, it's by permit only. One word of caution for boaters: Beware of the hydro plants just south of Artpark. There may be excellent fishing in their vicinity, but the tricky currents created by their water releases demand much attention along with adequate boat size and horsepower. Boats of less than 16 feet and 25 horsepower should not attempt to fish near these facilities.

For shoreline anglers, access is provided at Artpark in Lewiston, and at the Lewiston Sand Dock (Guard Park) at the end of Center Street. Fort Niagara also provides bank access along with the Joseph Davis State Park on Rt. #18 between Youngstown and Lewiston.

Further south towards the falls, fishing takes on an ever more adventurous posture. At Whirlpool State Park and Devil's Hole State Park one can take in the grandeur of the omnipresent Niagara Falls Gorge. Here, nimble footed fishermen make like rocky mountain sheep and descend steep canyon walls on steps leading to paths all along the lower river (life jackets and life lines help give a feeling of security). Also due to the hydro-electric generation, water level fluctuations must be constantly watched. However, the brave here are rewarded with many notable species including smallmouth bass and steelhead which can be caught along this wall all the way up to the Whirlpool Rapids Bridge.

Finally one comes to Lewiston, which bills itself as the "Smelt Capital of the World." It gets a tremendous run of these great-tasting little fish every spring, and anglers flock to Lewiston and catch smelt each night by the barrel full. Good places to dip a net include the Lewiston Sand Docks and Artpark near the bottom of the stairway by the observation tower.

East of the Niagara River is 12 Mile Creek which consists of two branches (East and West). The East Branch is most heavily fished and gets a good run of all major species. Excellent panfishing exists in both branches, with good runs of brown and rainbow trout each spring and fall. This is a non-snatching river! Fishing piers in Wilson and the Wilson-Tuscarora State Park off Route 18 offer easy access making these creeks very popular all summer long.

18 MILE CREEK

This is the largest stream, next to the awesome Niagara, in Niagara

County. It has an early run of spring steelhead, brown trout, and bullheads. As the days warm from spring to summer, hordes of panfish invade its inner reaches all the way up to Burt Dam, which is less than a mile from the lake proper. Smallmouth bass show for a while and largemouth bass take up permanent summer residence. Northern pike generally roam the creek and can be caught above and below the dam at Burt. Each fall, chinook and coho salmon return to the creek followed by the steelhead which remain all winter long.

Small boat fishing is very common and popular in this creek. Anglers drift through its slower sections from below the railroad bridge, through the gorge and all the way out to the inlet piers in Olcott. Fly fishermen and baitcasters also wade through much of this area below the railroad bridge where the creek flattens out and where steep canyon walls make it impossible to travel directly from the road to the river. Wading and drifting become the two best ways to utilize this weedy stretch.

Other access to this creek is gained from the Route 18 Bridge out to the piers in Olcott (only the western pier is open to the public). This is a popular area with bait fishermen casting for bass and panfish. Good catches of crappie, perch, silver bass, rock bass, and bullhead are made from late spring on through the entire summer. Fishing pressure on these species is generally low.

In the other direction from the railroad bridge to the dam, a distance just under a quarter of a mile, you can legally snatch Pacific salmon (chinook and coho only) each fall between August 15 and November 15 (always be sure to check current regulations). Steelhead, which usually enter the creek after November 15 for spawning, may not be snatched. Steelies are caught all along the river's course by both boat and wading fishermen.

In the rapid sections of creek between the bridge and dam, many good steelhead lies exist and fishermen do well casting flies, lures, and bait for the available fish. Of course, there's a big pool found directly beneath the Burt Dam which attracts considerable attention. Since the migratory species can't pass this point, the pool usually holds many of the fish found in the creek during any particular season and the majority of the fishermen, too.

The Niagara River is awesome and the Salmon River is phenomenal. But if you seek solitude you can find it on the lesser-known tributaries. Several of these exist between 18 Mile Creek and the

Genesee River, and in some Pacific salmon can be legally snatched from August 15 through November 15. Remember, it is strictly illegal to have any trout or salmon in your possession if fishing at night along any of these creeks.

The first is Oak Orchard Creek which enters the lake at Point Breeze. Trout and salmon can make it as far upstream as the Waterport Dam. The snagging zone runs from the Route 18 bridge upstream to the dam. Most action, however, is centered between the Lake Ontario State Parkway and the piers at Point Breeze.

Sandy Creek comes next. It offers good to excellent trout and salmon fishing upstream as far as the town of Murray. The snagging zone is located between the Lake Ontario Parkway Bridge upstream to the NY Rt. 104 bridge. Panfish are caught all over along with smallmouth bass and northern pike.

Following Sandy Creek comes Salmon Creek which enters Braddocks Bay. The legal snagging area runs from the Lake Ontario Parkway upstream to the impassable barrier at the dam above Parma Center Road. Because of all the posted, private lands alongs its banks, accessibility is limited to boats. Excellent trout and salmon runs are made each fall, and the creek has good populations of panfish, northerns, and smallmouth.

Special notice should be made of Slater Creek and Keg Creek, where snagging isn't allowed. Russell Station generating plant just outside the City of Rochester has a warm water discharge into Slater Creek. Great numbers of warm and cold water species are attracted to this discharge and anglers line the shore casting for brown trout, rainbow trout, and salmon. The creek and Little Round Pond usually remain ice free and fishable all winter long!

The significance of Keg Creek, which is located four miles east of Olcott Harbor, is that the DEC annually stocks steelhead in the creek and brown trout just offshore. Because this creek often dries up during the summer doesn't mean that it should be overlooked. When water is available, the creek averages about 10 feet wide with many interesting holding areas where you just might be all alone and find chinook, coho, browns, or steelhead. This "sleeper" is accessible from Route 18.

GENESEE RIVER·

This is a picture postcard river, flowing through the middle of the City of Rochester. If you're visiting the city, though, you may not see it, at least not unless you look down. The Genesee's northern six miles out to the lake are down deep inside a steep gorge. All the major Lake Ontario species are fished for in this gorge, or at the mouth of the river.

Major species available in season are rainbow and brown trout, coho and chinook salmon, smallmouth bass, some largemouth bass, channel catfish and bullhead, northern pike and panfish. There is a spring run of browns, rainbows, cohos, and chinooks.

Historically, the Genesee River was a well known salmon hot-spot. In his work "The Atlantic Salmon," Anthony Netboy indicates that men once fished for salmon here as they do today in Galway, Ireland. But, in 1817 Elisha Clark helped end the annual "land-locked salmon run" by building a dam at Rochester.

Today, snatching and blind snatching for Pacific salmon are legal from August 15 until November 15 from the Stutson River Bridge upstream to the first impassable barrier or the falls at the foot of Driving Park Avenue. You will note that the area just below the falls downstream to Seth Green Island gets very crowded. In spite of this, don't overlook the fishing potential of the rest of the river.

Trollers work this river for chinook salmon during October. They also troll very near the mouth of the Genesee west to the warm water discharge at the Russell Station. This is a late season hot-spot! Sometimes, there are so many chinook in this river, it's almost impossible not to catch one.

For boat fishermen, there are several good launching facilities. At the mouth of the river, in view of Charlottes Pier, is the Monroe County Public Boat Launch. Other boat access is gained via the NYS Genesee River Access Site off St. Paul Boulevard on the east side of the river. Good public access to the river is also gained here.

Remember, this river is accessible to a great many people who live right along its shores in the city. It is usually very well fished, but don't let that stop you. Try to get in on the annual smelt migration, the great panfishing off the piers, the late chinook salmon run, and the excellent winter steelheading.

IRONDEQUOIT CREEK

Once very polluted by municipal sewage, this creek has been cleaned up considerably, and the DEC now stocks large numbers of landlocked salmon and other salmonoids. Along with landlocks, each winter more and more steelhead seem to return, prompting

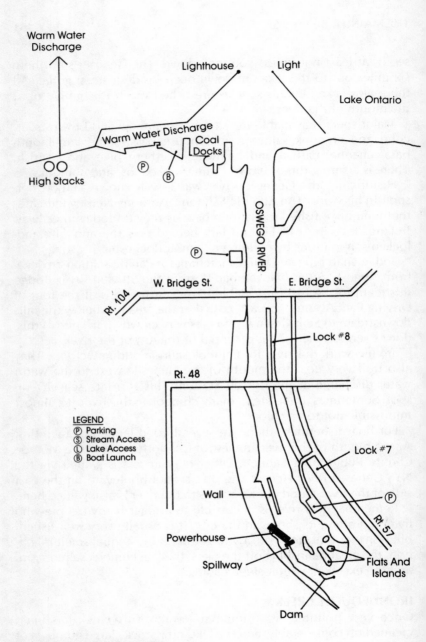

▶ *17b. THE OSWEGO RIVER*

increased angler activity.

Because the creek is in the experimental stages of landlocked salmon restoration, fishing is not allowed from October 1st until November 30th to protect the spawning fish. However, the first day or two after this creek reopens the fishermen descend in droves.

There's access to Irondequoit Creek at several locations. Cartop boats can put in at the Canoe and Cartop Access Site on Route 404. Ellison Park is accessed along Browncroft Blvd. or Blossom Road. You can also fish the creek in Penfield Linear Park which can be accessed from Rt. 441. Besides trout and salmon, bullhead, northern pike (which run the river to spawn every spring) and panfish are available.

As we've mentioned at other points, you do not have to stick to the Salmon River to make excellent stream catches. Some of the other less-fished streams are between Irondequoit Creek and the Oswego River. Included in the list are some where snatching of Pacific Salmon is allowed from August 15 until November 15. These streams are Sodus Creek from Ridge Road upstream to the first impassable barrier at NY Rt. 104 and Sterling Valley Creek from the bridge at Fraden Road upstream to the impassable barrier at N.Y. Rt. 104.

Along with these waters, you may want to try fishing a few of the lesser streams such as the Salmon Creek in Pultneyville, Maxwell Creek just west of Sodus Bay, and Wolcott Creek exiting Port Bay. Although these waters aren't directly stocked with Pacific salmon or steelhead, these fish often do stray in. Should there be much rain or a good runoff, steelhead will most definitely appear. Panfish, bass, and northern pike are also available.

OSWEGO RIVER

Overlooked for many years, the Oswego River was a well kept secret of area residents. These knowledgeable locals annually bypassed the more crowded Salmon River to the north for the bountiful waters they found right in their own backyard. A short river, the Oswego wasn't always that way. Once, the mighty landlocked salmon could roam from the big lake all the way upstream to Baldwinsville, New York. But soon after a canal had been built between Oswego and Syracuse in the late 1800's, the salmon died out.

Netboy also points out that as early as 1654 the Jesuit Fathers

► *A gathering of trophy brown trout hunters at the Oswego River spillway.*

Le Moyne and Le Mercier reported seeing red men coming down the Oswego River in canoes filled with salmon. They further indicated that there were so many fish that you could actually kill them with a paddle.

What, then, is the modern day salmon potential of the river? The DEC stocks this short (½ mile) tributary with steelhead and brown trout, and coho and chinook salmon, while offshore brown and lake trout are planted into the lake proper. The steelhead, cohos, and chinook all mount excellent runs into the river in season. As for the browns, they seem to have found a home in this river and can be caught 12 months of the year. Lake trout rarely venture into the river, but are caught offshore in 51 degrees of water in good numbers throughout the year.

In the harbor at the mouth of the Oswego, tremendous panfishing delights the young and old. All along the shoreline there is a chain-linked fence in front of which anglers cast for a multitude of species. Catfish, freshwater drum, walleyes, smallmouth bass, and rock bass are all taken in good numbers.

Upstream of the inlet, you quickly go under two traffic bridges and come to a series of locks, canals, dams, and a giant spillway where many brown trout and salmon are caught annually. At the spillway, it isn't too uncommon to see anglers with quite a large mixed bag. American shad, walleyes, brown trout, coho salmon, and chinook salmon all seem to run the river from mid-September through October. In November, the coho and chinook slowly part the scene, while the steelhead makes its annual return.

Look for good to excellent catches from the dam area where a series of rock islands allow you to cross the river beneath the dam. You are also allowed up on the lower skirt of the dam where many anglers connect with giant chinook salmon. One word of caution: Often, water may begin coming over the dam without any warning! When this happens and when they open up the powerhouse 100 yards away by the spillway, the river will rise. Many anglers panic when this happens. Some climb trees, others attempt to climb the high concrete wall; however, even though it gets very scary, an adult will have little problem crossing the river to the parking lot on the other side.

Should the river be high, simply take up position along its banks, and begin casting. Across from the spillway, drift baits or cast lures. Up at the dam, drift spawn bags. If you can cross the river, fish worms and spawn bags in the shoot coming down the spillway. This has made a very deep hole and if you can get your bait down into it, chances are good you will catch a brown trout. As for salmon, anglers cast towards the powerplant and attempt to catch chinook salmon which can actually be seen swimming.

This is an easy river to fish. It is rather short, and it has tremendous potential. If you have never caught a king salmon, and are afraid of the fast moving currents in other tributaries try to fish the Oswego River sometime between mid-September and late October.

Between the Oswego River and the Salmon River, you can try in Catfish Creek, Butterfly Creek, the Little Salmon River, and Grindstone Creek. Each of these gets a run of trout and salmon. Northern pike, smallmouth bass, rock bass, catfish, and other panfish are in good supply.

THE SALMON RIVER

The Salmon River poses a dilemma: It is the best Lake Ontario tributary but it is also the most crowded. Further, a first timer here will have difficulty finding his way around. There are many places to fish and the names of the more familiar spots seem to all blend together. Even if the first timer fishes with a knowledgeable guide, he has a hard time orienting himself to the locations he is fishing.

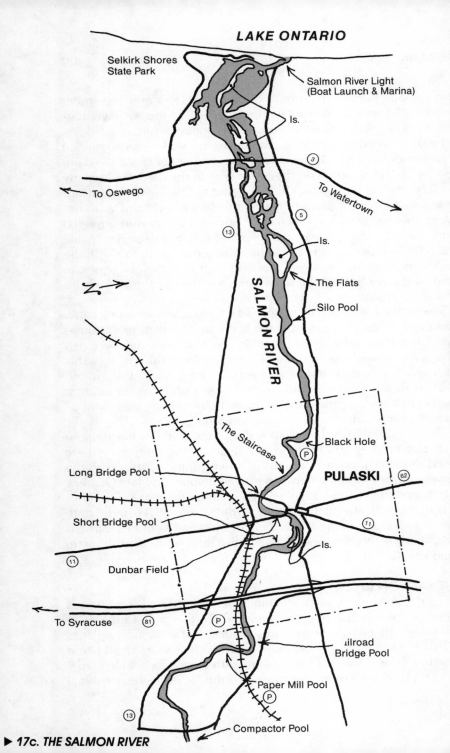

▶ 17c. THE SALMON RIVER

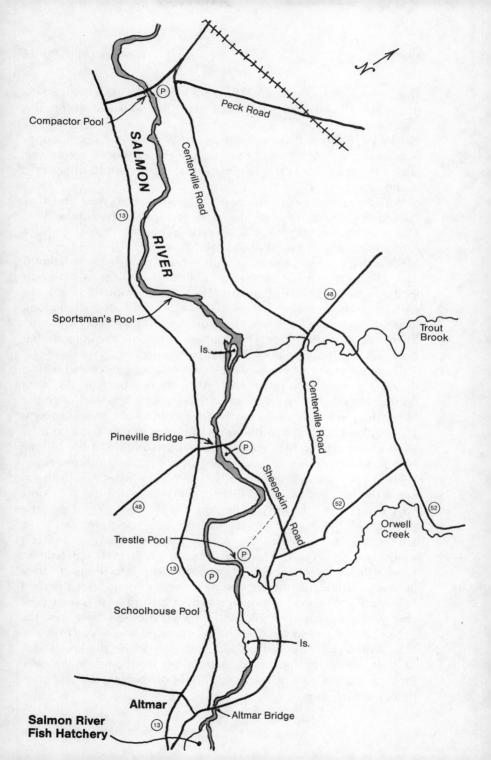

The accompanying map, Fig. 17-c, will help you a great deal. Study this map (as well as an area road map) and you will eventually become Salmon River literate.

Take the Salmon River map in this book and set it down along-side a New York State road map. Locate the Salmon River on the large road map. Study the two maps making certain to orient one to the other.

Notice that the river runs basically from east to west and that Pulaski sits almost in the middle of the fishable portion of the river. This is an important fact. You are either between Pulaski and the Altmar hatchery or Pulaski and Lake Ontario.

For many, Pulaski is the main starting point for fishing the Salmon River. There are several good spots right in the village and they go by the names of Long Bridge Pool, Short Bridge Pool, and the Stair-case Pool. The easist way to get to these locations is to travel along Route 13 to Route 11. Travel north on Route 11 and you will cross the river and Short Bridge. Downstream of this are the Long Bridge Pool and the Staircase Pool in rapid succession.

These pools are often crowded. However, during steelhead season they are sometimes underfished. Also, do not pass up this area during times of high water. Most anglers vacate the river once the water flow from the upstream Hydro-electric Dam reaches town. This high water time can fluctuate from day to day, but as a rule, you can expect the high water to reach the middle of the Village of Pulaski somewhere around 11 AM from Monday through Friday.

Fish these town pools carefully! There are always fish in them. Since the big flood in the winter of 1985, many of the old pools have been changed. One good example is Staircase Pool. Once the river just glided along over very shallow shale rock, but now, there are deep pools cut out of the river bottom. Fish each pool as if it was opening day on your favorite trout stream. Even though Salmon River fish are large, once they get down deep into the pools they are very difficult if not impossible to see. Pretend that there's a fish waiting wherever you would expect a trout and you may be rewarded with something bigger than what you have bargained for.

Now, this is not to say that the experienced angler can't see the fish. With a pair of polarized sun glasses and with the knowledge of what to look for, you can most definitely see the fish in the river. Pick up a good pair of those essential polaroid glasses and then practice using them.

Downstream of the Staircase Pool you come to the Black Hole. This is another heavily fished pool, but on occasion, I have had the entire pool to myself. Don't dismiss it sight unseen.

Still further downstream are the Little Black Hole, Silo Pool, The Flats, and finally the Clay Pool. During the steelhead and salmon season many anglers park in the Lake Street parking lot and fish this area heavily. Understand that this area will always be crowded.

The other direction you can head from Pulaski is east. Again, refer to Fig. 17-c. Get on Centerville Road, traveling east, and you will eventually come to a railroad crossing. There is parking on both sides of the road at this point. By walking in along the tracks you come to the river. Standing high above the river on a trestle and looking east you will see Papermill Pool and to your west will be Railroad Bridge Pool. Though well fished, these pools are seldom crowded.

Further east, you come to Compactor Pool. Many people fish for a good distance upstream on both sides of the river at this location. There is a large fisherman's parking lot here, and most drift boat captains make this the point at which they pull out their boats. Continuing across the bridge, you will be back on Route 13. If you make a right, you will return to the McDonald's in town; but by going left, you will soon come to the most popular section of this river, one called Sportsman's Pool.

From the parking lot out on Rt. 13 it is a good walk into the pool, especially if there's much snow or ice on the ground. Anglers spread out all along both banks, and the pool can accommodate over 50 fishermen. Steelhead, coho, and chinook are all taken in good numbers.

Still further east you come to Pineville. By making a left in the center of this small town, you will cross the Pineville Bridge. This is the lower limit of the Salmon River snatching area (Pacific salmon only). From here on upstream to the Altmar Bridge, a distance of about two miles, snatching hooks are legal from August 15 until October 15. All other species of fish accidentally snagged in this section (as well as elsewhere) must be released immediately.

After crossing over the bridge, make a right onto Sheepskin Road. You will come after about ¾'s of a mile to a heavily traveled dirt road on your right. If you take this road to its end, you will come to Trestle Pool. This is another popular location and most times you will see hordes of anglers blind snatching salmon or legally fishing for steelhead trout.

Snatching and blind snatching are very popular here. In fact this short snagging section plays host to, at times, hundreds (if not thousands) of anglers. At the same time, the long stretch from the Pineville Bridge out to the big lake (which is much longer) will have only half the number of fishermen. It can still get very crowded, though.

Up from the Trestle Pool is the Village of Altmar. Here you will find Schoolhouse Pool. This pool is the favorite of most knowledgeable steelhead anglers in the area. It's very long and deep. Many steelhead and salmon are caught. Also, should it snow you can try right at the Altmar Bridge which is the most upstream location where you can legally fish.

RIVER FISHING TACTICS

"As you're wading, you'll see salmon of such a tremendous size swimming by you'll think they can knock you over. Don't laugh. It's happened."

▼
18

If you were to join end to end all the creeks, rivers, and streams that run into Lake Ontario, you would have one very long river offering every conceivable type of river fishing possibility. You would encounter slow and fast moving sections, waterfalls, boulder-strewn areas, broad expanses featuring many different pools and pockets, deep pools, long glides, placid pond-like pools, white water rapids, long elbow pools, and staircase pools. You would find a myriad of fish holdings locations, such as stream junctions, undercut banks, railroad abutments that divide the river, fallen trees that offer sanctuary, and river currents that have created deep channels running through seemingly simple pools. In the previous chapter we looked at the physical characteristics of the tributaries large and small that empty into Lake Ontario on the U.S. side. Now let's look at some specific fishing techniques and apply them in detail to the associated species.

GEARING UP FOR MONSTER SALMON

From early September on through October is a time of much anticipation on the tributaries leading into Lake Ontario. This is when the titanic salmon make their annual spawning run.

As you're wading, you'll see salmon of such a tremendous size swimming by you'll think they can knock you over. Don't laugh — it's happened. Although several species of fish are pursued now, head and shoulders above the others is the chinook or "king" salmon. Chinooks of 15-35 pounds are taken daily, while the cohos caught right along with them average 8-15 pounds.

The kings are not easily caught once they enter the rivers. Nonetheless, they can be taken, and salmon egg clusters seem to make the most tempting bait. Use heavy salmon fishing tackle (fly or spinning), nothing less than 17-pound test line (unless you don't mind breaking off a few fish) and sturdy salmon hooks. Fly rods must be powerful or they will not be able to stand up to the tremendous pressure applied by a large, fleeting fish. These brutes can snap 20 lb. test line like it was mere sewing thread, so drag systems must be working perfectly.

If you are more interested in catching coho or trout, both smaller than the chinook, use light to medium salmon tackle. Light fly rods will be in order to provide maximum sport. Although you can also catch the larger chinooks on such tackle, the typically crowded stream conditions mandate tackle heavy enough to control the fish.

Match your gear to the fish: Big tackle for big chinooks, lighter tackle for the other species.

SUCCESSFUL SALMON TECHNIQUES & BAITS

While out in the lake, salmon are decidedly nighttime feeders. When they first enter the tributaries, they retain this propensity (even though they stop feeding completely as they move upstream). On the tribs, then, most success is had by anglers fishing at dawn and again at dusk. The moment other anglers start competing over a pool of fish, you can pretty much call it a day. The fish will become very line shy, and will be unlikely to strike.

Salmon fresh in from the lake like swift current and show a fondness for bright colored spawn bags. Good salmon holding areas include elbow pools, undercut banks, pocket pools, boulder strewn water, pools behind abutments, eddies, or under waterfalls. You should thoroughly scout the river for such pools and make note to fish them at daybreak the following morning or at dusk. Bright orange, green or red make the best spawn bag colors.

Another bait that has taken salmon when fished early in the morning is the strung shiner. Hook a three inch shiner onto a double needle hook using 17-pound test line. Once rigged, drift the shiner into a salmon holding pool and allow it to compete for space with the huge salmon. Sometimes, a big fish will take exception to the little fish and strike in an attempt to move it out of the pool. Should this happen, hang on!

Big salmon hooked legally in this manner rarely jump. They just head off very rapidly either up or downstream. All you can do at this point is apply pressure and try to follow the fish as it tears along from pool to pool. In most stretches anglers are very cooperative and will give way to a simple call of "fish on." Eventually, the big fish will slow down and you will be able to catch up to it. However, the fight may not be over.

What you should do at this point is get a tight reign on the fish and try to make it swim upstream. In so doing, it will be fighting both you and the current. If you can keep it headed in this direction, it will only be a matter of time until you can swim him up on the beach (the preferred method of landing a huge salmon). You can expect the average battle to last between 10-20 minutes.

With smaller chinook and cohos, which may be in the river along with the giants, expect many good jumps but a much shorter fight.

▶ *Some anglers don't adapt well to crowding. Expect it on many of the bigger tribs, and especially on the Salmon River.*

Since these fish weigh on the average of 8-15 pounds, the basic giant salmon tackle will usually whip them quickly. However, you will be amazed at how fast and acrobatic they are.

When fishing very early in the morning, it's impossible to fish for any particular species. That is, each pool is likely to contain a little of everything. Once you get yourself into position, start drifting your bait into the pool. The most aggressive fish should investigate and strike. Often this fish will be a brown trout. Regardless of what fish initiates the action, your chances of catching a salmon remain good until the sun rises or until other anglers start coming to your pool. Should you hook into a coho, your line will dart all around as if caught in a whirlpool, and there will probably be some aerial acrobatics thrown in. If you want to eat your catch, then by all means keep the coho! However, if you want a wall fish, you may want to release these smaller fish.

When fishing the Salmon River, it is advised you call the Salmon River (Pulaski) Water Level Status: (315) 298-6531. Information given will indicate when the river will be high, that is, when the power plant will be running and releasing water into the river. It's absolutely impossible to know when the river will be up without first consulting this source.

Should the power plant run normal hours, 8 a.m. until 4 p.m., you can expect daily high water from 11 a.m. on. This is good, because fresh salmon will be entering the river all during periods of high water and will be available for you to catch during both periods of high and low water conditions. In recent years, the power plant has even released water on weekends. This makes it rather difficult for the individual who likes to fish low water conditions. But if you are lucky and the water is down when you arrive or even during your time on the river, you can expect to find pools of salmon just waiting for you.

It was about an hour before sunrise when "Rosey" Hughes and I, both carrying flashlights, made our way down the steep canyon walls toward the Salmon River. It was pitch black, and without the lights you couldn't see a foot in front of your face. We had left our car in the Lake Street parking lot and we were on our way to fish the Flats (see Fig. 17-c). They are located about 500 yards south of the river access site. Upon safely reaching the bottom of the cliff, we could see with our weak lights and hear that the river was low (they weren't releasing water from the reservoir).

"Follow me," I called to Rosey as I headed across an ankle deep section of the river.

We knew that we couldn't fish for the big bruisers for still another half hour, but we also knew that if we were to stand a chance on a few giant chinooks we had better be in place before the crowd arrived.

After about 10 minutes of walking along the bank, Rosey interrupted the silence and said, "I'm going to cross the river and fish right there." He motioned towards a long, deep pool which ran along an undercut bank just above where the old Clay Pool had been (the river changes from year to year).

"I'm going to fish among the boulders just ahead some," I replied to Rosey. "I saw a few fish splashing up into that area a few minutes ago."

Once I got into position, I could see a few huge backs of several salmon. They were finning in the current just below a large boulder that was causing a steady stream of water to shoot in their direction. I got well above the fish and promptly set about stringing a shiner on the end of my 17-pound test line. Rosey called across the river that we still had about five minutes to wait.

When the right time arrived, it was beginning to get light and other anglers could be seen making their way along the banks. Rosey was fishing a bright colored spawn bag and quickly tied into a salmon. I could see him following the fish downstream as it splashed about 100 feet ahead of him. I slowly began paying out line and working my shiner into position.

No sooner had my bait reached the finning fish when, "pow," I felt a strong tug on the end of my 9-foot salmon fly rod. I quickly pulled back, but missed the fish. But before the sick feeling could set in, another salmon grabbed hold. Now, both Rosey and I were headed downstream fighting fish.

We were both successful and managed to beach two salmon that went well over 30 pounds apiece. But when we returned to where we had hooked up, we knew that our fishing was over for a while. There were anglers all along the river. In salmon fishing, the very early bird gets the fish and luckily we had gotten ours.

"Let's try some smaller creeks this morning," Rosey suggested.

"Good idea," I called back, "we can always come back here around 11 AM after the water's come up and the crowds are gone,"

Keep in mind that after the river rises, most anglers call it a day and you can have the entire river to yourself. When this happens, I have several locations that I like and can still fish. True, it's very difficult. Once a big fish is hooked and gets out into the fast current, it's next to impossible to stop it. So lines break and few fish are landed. But there's no crowd, and with the fish moving upstream, there's little difficulty in presenting your bait to many passing fish.

Other salmon techniques such as lifting and snatching have areas of many rivers set aside for them. Detailed descriptions of these techniques are given in Ch. 14. Also, make certain to be aware of the different tackle restrictions applied to the Salmon River including the Salmon River rig (see Fig. 18-b).

LURES FOR SALMON

Salmon not only strike bait, but also on occasion lures. Two of the most popular ones in this region are the Hotshot and Little Cleo. With the Hotshot, you should use the drop back method where you stand at the head of a pool and float the lure downstream to where you want it to fish. Then, engage your reel and allow the lure to

TRIBUTARY	LOCATION	COUNTY
Four Mile Creek	Between Fort Niagara & Wilson	Niagara
Six Mile Creek	Between Fort Niagara & Wilson	Niagara
Twelve Mile Creek	Wilson	Niagara
Golden Hill Creek	Golden Hill State Park	Niagara
Keg Creek	Four miles east of Olcott Harbor	Niagara
Johnson Creek	Lake side Park	Orleans
Oak Orchard Creek	Point Breeze	Orleans
Sandy Creek	North Hamlin	Monroe
Salmon Creek	Braddock Point	Monroe
Salmon Creek	Pultneyville	Wayne
Marshall Creek	Sodus Point	Wayne
Wolcott Creek	Wolcott	Wayne
Sterling Creek	Fair Haven	Cayuga
Catfish Creek	Demster	Oswego
Butterfly Creek	Between Texas & Demster	Oswego
Little Salmon Creek	Texas	Oswego
Grindstone Creek	Port Ontario	Oswego
Little Sandy Creek	Sandy Pond	Oswego
Lindsey Creek	North Pond	Jefferson
Skinner Creek	North Pond	Jefferson
South Sandy Creek	Ellisburg	Jefferson
Sandy Creek	Woodville	Jefferson
Black River	Dexter	Jefferson
Perch River	Limerick	Jefferson
Chaumont River	Depauville	Jefferson

▶ 18a. MINOR TRIBUTARIES TO LAKE ONTARIO — From Niagara to Cape Vincent dig deeply down into the current. Salmon don't feed during their spawning run, but the vibrations and position of the little lure will often annoy a fish enough to prompt it to "chase" the lure out of the pool. When this occurs, strike immediately.

As for the Little Cleos, you will see them fished where anglers have a large concentration of salmon swimming around in a pocket of water in a non-snatching section (such as beneath the power plant in the Oswego River). Here, fishermen cast Cleos with rather low expectations of a salmon actually chasing and striking the lure. Rather, they expect to illegally snag a fish as the lure passes through the crowd. Sometimes the lure actually succeeds in hooking the fish in the mouth. When this happens, it's classified as a legal catch. Salmon hooked anywhere in the body in a non-snatching section must be released, unharmed, immediately.

As for chinook chasing and seizing a lure in this type of situation, it doesn't happen often. Once Rosey was fishing alongside an out-of-uniform (but not off duty) game warden. The officer was casting a Little Cleo into the Oswego River across from the power plant when a big salmon came up and visibly grabbed his lure. Rosey informed the angler that he didn't think a salmon would actually grab a lure once it had entered the river. At this time, the "angler" revealed that he was, in fact, a warden (wardens often go under-cover) and that during the past seven years of fishing the tributaries almost every day during the salmon season, this was the first big salmon that he could actually recall taking one of his lures.

YEAR ROUND TROUT FISHING
Whereas giant chinook salmon provide excellent fishing from September through October, trout are available in many tributaries year round. During the winter, they can be caught off piers near the mouth of rivers. As the season progresses, they readily move upstream where, for the most part, they reside in the upper reaches of the tributaries (except in the Niagara, where they're all over). Many of the trout residing in these rivers will have been stocked in them. These fish will be smaller, from 8-12 inches, and will have no migratory instinct to travel down to the big lake. Lake fish will enter the river to either spawn or feed on the roe of other fish and they will be larger, from 3-20 pounds.

The "upper reaches" of a tributary doesn't have to mean too far removed from the lake, either. When you're far enough upstream that the river becomes wadable and a current is distinguishable, trout become available. In these river reaches, you'd be wise to drift your bait under floats or directly along the bottom (see Fig. 19-b — Basic Float and Basic Trout Rig). Brown trout, domestic rainbow, brook trout, steelhead trout — all these species respond well to drifted baits. These handsome fish all make formidable adversaries too, especially when caught on light tackle. Here are some of their favorite baits and ways to present each.

Trout up to twenty pounds can be caught on garden worms, meal worms, hellgrammites, nightcrawlers, caddisworms, and salamanders. Thread the bait on size #8-12 bait holder hooks, then add enough split-shot to get the bait down and still enable it to drift. While fishing bait, chubs become a constant nuisance. Found in all streams, these prime northern and musky baits are impossible to avoid. If they become too numerous where you are fishing, move to a new section. For other bait choices refer to Fig. 4-a.

Line as light as two pound test — for the smaller trout — in combination with a casting bubble makes an excellent way to drift bait without always getting hung up on bottom. Use a single, light split-shot and allow the bait to drift along in the current, preferably about one foot above the bottom. Of course, as the size of the fish increases, go with progressively heavier line.

Another highly effective trout bait is the minnow. Fished on a size #8 hook, simply bring the hook up through both the lower and upper lips and cast across the stream. Allow the minnow to swing back around downstream. Then, slowly retrieve it back to your position. Or if you want, you can wade down the middle of the stream and fish the minnow out from each bank. Minnows are lethal on large brown and rainbow trout.

Salmon eggs or egg clusters fished on a small size #10 salmon egg hook also make deadly bait. If using single eggs, use only one egg per hook. Make certain to hide the hook entirely by running it around the inside of the egg. A single light split-shot on two pound test line is preferred, but four pound test can also get the job done.

For aquatic insects, use no heavier than two pound test line and no bigger than a size #12 baitholder hook. Fish this bait, as with salmon eggs, in white water sections of rivers, shallow fast moving rapids, and beneath waterfalls. At such locations, trout are fooled into thinking that the current has dislodged something good to eat from the bottom.

Trout family members also respond well to lures. Some of the best spinning lures are silver or gold in color. Using sizes #0-2, cast the lure across the stream and retrieve it with a slow and steady motion.

Some proven spinning lures for trout include the C.P. Swing, Mepps, Phoebe, Little Cleo, Rooster Tail, Panther Martin, and Blue Fox Spinners. One important thing to remember about fishing these lures is that the colder the water is, the slower the lure should be retrieved. This is because the cold water slows the fish's metabolism, and so it has less energy available to chase lures.

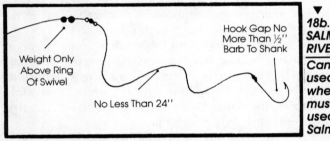

▼
**18b.
SALMON
RIVER RIG**

Can be used any-where but must be used in the Salmon River.

(within image) Weight Only Above Ring Of Swivel

(within image) Hook Gap No More Than ½" Barb To Shank

(within image) No Less Than 24"

FLY-FISHING FOR TROUT

When fly fishing for trout, a good 8 - 8½ foot fly rod for 6 or 7 weight line is recommended. With such a versatile combination, you can fish a multitude of flies intended for every species of fish found in these rivers. Almost every baitfish, aquatic insect and terrestrial flying insect has a particular pattern designed for it, so your choice of imitations can include nymphs, wet flies, dry flies and streamers.

A major portion of a trout's diet is aquatic insects, thus artificials that imitate mayflies, caddis flies, midges, and stoneflies are basic to the serious angler's arsenal. It is often (though not always) important to match the hatch (use a fly similar to what the fish are feeding on) to catch fish. Fly fishermen should use light, tapered 7½-9 foot leaders. Use a 4X-6X tippet for the smaller trout, but a

heavier leader up to 6 lb. test for larger fish. For wet flies, nymphs, and streamers use sinking weight forward fly lines. For dry flies, stick to double tapered or weight forward floating lines.

Some old, respected nymph or nymph-like patterns are the Zug Bug, Caddis Larva, Pink and Brown Scud, Hare's Ear, and Stone Fly. For wet flies try the Professor, Light Cahill, Royal Coachman, Hare's Ear, or Black Gnat. When the fish are freely rising use dry flies to match the hatch wherever possible. Some tested dry fly patterns include the Blue Dun, Light Hendrickson, Light and Dark Cahill, Royal Coachman, and Adams. Good streamers and bucktails include the Gray Ghost, Black Nosed Dace, White Marabou, Mickey Finn, Olive Matuka, Muddler Minnow, and Supervisor. Streamer patterns are usually size #4-10. Dry flies and wets range from size #8 all the way down to size #22 and smaller depending upon what's hatching.

Although good spinning for trout exists year round, good fly fishing usually runs from late May on through September. Of course, winter steelhead fishing allows the dedicated fly fisherman to pursue his sport for the entire winter. (Unfortunately, during the much shorter autumn salmon season, flies seldom work and are not much used). Regardless of what type of fly fishing you enjoy — whether it be small trout on an ultra-light fly rod or much larger trout on sturdier tackle — there's room for you and your style of fishing on one of the tributaries emptying into Lake Ontario.

A MIXED BAG LIKE YOU'VE NEVER SEEN

Should you tie into a brown or rainbow trout while fishing in the rivers for salmon, don't expect it to be anything too small. During the salmon season, big trout follow spawning salmon into the rivers and it's not uncommon to catch a few of these fish in excess of 10 pounds. In fact, many anglers fish specifically for trout during this period. Once, while fishing in the "little Black Hole" on the Salmon River using 12 pound test line for salmon, Joe Rosa, Mike Kersey and I caught several brown and rainbow trout that were big, beautiful, and over eight pounds each. We released each one of these fish because we were more interested in catching a few of the giant chinook salmon we could see swimming in the pool. When you're hunting a 40-pound salmon, little 10 pound browns or rainbows just get in the way. (Before fishing Lake Ontario, I would never have believed that I could make such an outrageous statement — and mean it!)

It you want to fish specifically for these larger browns, the best place to catch them is in deep river pools or pockets. Mixed in with the browns, you may occasionally find a lone rainbow. The best bait for these larger trout is a freshly tied spawn bag, but worms, lures, and streamer flies can also turn the trick. Perhaps the most important ingredient for consistent catches is light line. One word of advice here: Go as light as you have to. If that means using four pound test, do it. But for the most part, six to eight pound test line will be as low as you will have to go.

Some good places to catch big browns during late September and October include the lower reaches of the Salmon River, the Oswego River, and Eighteen Mile Creek. These rivers are all heavily fished for salmon during this period and it's not too uncommon to have a trout pool all to yourself.

WARM WATER SURPRISES

For northern pike and muskellunge use either large shiners or large 6-8 inch chubs. Fish them 2-4 feet under a float, using a size #4/0 or #2/0 bait holder hook or chub harness (see Fig. 19-b). Use an eight-inch wire leader between line and hook or harness, and position a clamp-on weight 6-10 inches above the wire leader. Frogs and Salamanders can also be used for these species, and are best fished on weedless bass hooks (see Fig. 19-b). Fish salamanders on the bottom or frogs along with a float. Nightcrawlers are often effective, too. They are best fished about one foot above the bottom or above weedbeds. Use #2/0 bait holder hooks and 12-inch wire leaders. Fish them under a float or along with a heavy weight and float combination off the bottom (again, see Fig. 19-b).

I can remember one episode that occurred while I was fishing with Mike Kersey near the Rt. 3 bridge which crosses the Salmon River at Port Ontario. A big northern pike came up and grabbed a live frog that was intended for a large bass we had seen surfacing in the area. I wasn't using any wire and so I lost the fish during its initial run. If you're interested in northerns, always use a short wire leader, regardless of the bait you have on. If there's a possibility of a northern striking a bait intended for bass, go with a heavy monofilament leader. This works well early in the morning, when the bass can't see it. As the day brightens, though, fish progressively lighter leaders for bass.

Northerns and muskies can also be caught quite readily on big lures, but make certain that your hooks are all razor sharp. When a big northern or musky grabs hold of a lure, your rod must be powerful enough to really set these hooks into the fish's bony mouth. Otherwise, the big fish will open its mouth and out will pop the lure!

Some favorite pike family spinning lures include the Mepp's Muskie Killer, Blue Fox Super Vibrax Buck, Pike Harasser, Smity Ruslur, and Musky Harasser. For spinnerbaits, use double tandem spinners like the Tinsel Tail or Musky Tandem. The Rocker Buzzer and Weed Eater are two highly recommended buzzbaits.

If using plugs, try the Smity Baits, Teddy Baits, Jointed Smity, Swicks, Jointed Pikie, and Swim Whizz crankbaits. These are all big lures that should be fished along the surface (if floaters) or about three feet under the water and over rocky bottom in slow moving currents for muskies. Northerns, on the other hand, have a strong tendency to come out from the weeds, so fish the baits very close to weedbeds that might make potential holding areas.

Finally, pike, pickerel, and musky love to strike spoons. Over the years the red and white Daredevle has been a favorite. Just cast and retrieve, and the long, toothy critters should do the rest.

CATCHING STEELHEAD

"Although I've caught thousands of fish, the 15-pound steelhead left me shaking for 20 minutes. Its line-stripping runs were simply dazzling."

19

Steelhead rank among the most exciting fish caught anywhere in the world They grow strong and big — 23 lb. 5 oz. is the current NYS Record. Should a 10-pounder (just an average steelie) grab your bait or lure while the water is still warm, perhaps during the latter part of October, a tremendous battle will ensue. Runs of up to 100 yards, breathtaking leaps, and arduous bulldogging sessions all characterize the typical 10-15 minute ordeal.

As the water cools, the power of the fish can still be recognized, but the length of the runs and duration of the battle by mid-winter will most definitely be affected. The cold water may dampen the steelhead's overall fighting ability, but it does little to damper his aggressive striking spirit. All winter long, wherever open water exists in the tributaries to Lake Ontario, hardy anglers almost religiously make steelhead pilgrimages to the mecca.

In this chapter, we will name Lake Ontario's better steelhead producing tributaries. We will discuss basic steelhead rigs and how to prepare, preserve and use effective baits. We'll talk about how to select and use steelhead lures, and how to prepare for a typical late-fall, early-spring driftboat trip.

WHERE TO FISH

By all means if you have never witnessed the incredible raw power and natural beauty of the Niagara Falls, plan to do it this winter. Seeing the entire falls encrusted in massive snow and ice formations, at night displayed by colored lights, is an unparalleled thrill. But better yet for fishermen, the gorge and river below will be literally crawling with steelhead.

The lower Niagara River is a broad and fast-moving expanse of water. Although it slows down some near the town of Lewiston, even here bank and boat anglers alike must maintain a levelheaded respect for its treacherous currents. Like the Salmon River far to the east, this is a hydro-electric power producing river which has periods of safe, low water conditions before the power is generated. After the turbines begin to churn, sometime around 8 AM daily, the river rises and anglers must be ever cautious not to get caught up in the increased current and ensuing high waters.

As for steelhead fishing, the river is a A-One! Bank fishermen cast spawn bags and lures between Art Park and the Whirlpool Rapids Bridge, off the Lewiston Sand Docks, along the river south of Spire, and at the Youngstown docks. Boat fishermen troll lures and drift baits everywhere all winter long. For all references to the Niagara, see Fig. 17-a in Ch. 17.

At the mouth of the river, about 6½ fishable miles north of the falls, sits Fort Niagara. Driving east from the fort, you travel along Route 18, toward Rochester, and encounter one potential steelhead stream after another. On nice days (with open water available), you can fish at inlets or in rivers and creeks found along the way for steelhead, brown or lake trout. Be warned, though, that during the steelhead season all sections of this lake are subject to snow squalls and white outs. These unpredictable storms often last for hours and make driving conditions hazardous or impossible. These squalls, along with the ever-constant threat of day long snow falls and bitterly cold temperatures make steelheading here a true test of man against nature.

The first two steelhead rivers east of the fort are Four and Six Mile Creeks. They are rarely fished but usually do harbor some steelhead during the winter. Further along the route is Twelve Mile Creek, which enters Lake Ontario by the Town of Wilson. Here, steelhead are caught at the inlet off the east pier or along the river, if open.

Eighteen Mile Creek at Olcott provides another excellent inlet and river, and steelhead here can be caught all the way back to Burt Dam when the river is ice free. When the river is frozen, try fishing off the stone pier at the inlet.

You can get to the pier by walking down the short path found at the end of Van Buren Street in the middle of Olcott on the western side of the river. Cut across the beach and you will be on the pier. Fish spawn bags, single salmon eggs, or worms on the bottom for steelhead and brown trout, both of which are usually quite active all winter long at this location. If you can get into the river, fish beneath Burt Dam. There's ample parking for anglers at Fisherman's Park in Burt from which it's only a short walk downhill to the river and upstream to the dam.

Olcott is a fisherman's village. It may be locked up tighter than a drum during a severe winter, but for most of the year it's the hub of area salmon and steelhead fishing. Beyond Olcott comes Golden Hill Creek with access at Golden Hill State Park off Route 18, Marsh Creek where you can fish at both the Routes 18 and 104 bridges, and Johnson's Creek with access along Yates-Carlton Townline Road and at Lakeside Beach State Park.

Moving east you come to Keg Creek, which is very lightly fished and which has a good run of steelhead when the creek is high. Next comes Oak Orchard Creek where you can catch steelhead along the lower section. The best time of year here is early in the spring or after a good thaw or heavy rain sometime around late march or early April. Access is gained at the Route 18 bridge for the lower section. After this comes Sandy Creek in North Hamlin where you can fish along Route 19 whenever the river is open.

Continuing east, you come to Salmon Creek out of Braddocks Bay. Steelies are caught here annually. Best times are in the late fall and early spring. Again, spawn bags, individual salmon eggs, worms and wigglers are the best baits. Look for access along Route 18 east of Hilton.

After this, you get on the Lake Ontario State Parkway and eventually come to the Genesee River in Rochester. The Genesee is a broad, deep river that yields excellent catches of steelhead. Fish below the falls at Driving Park Avenue all the way out to the lake and off Charlotte's pier (the western pier) at the inlet. This is a beautiful river that runs down a deep gorge right through the middle of the city. During the warmer months, however, the river can be rather foul smelling and on many occasions actually warrants a wide berth.

East of the Genesee, you can fish off the two new jetties guarding the inlet at Irondequoit Bay. Also try Irondequoit Creek, at one time rather polluted, but now reclaimed and an excellent fall, winter, and spring steelhead fishing creek. Fish can be caught as far upstream as the town of Fishers. If adequate water's available, don't overlook the steelhead fishing potential of Allen's Creek.

Steelhead can be caught off the pier in Webster, out of Salmon Creek in Pultneyville and from Maxwell Creek just this side of Sodus Bay. These last two creeks are small and slow moving. You can only fish them during mild weather (spring and fall) and during periods of high water.

At Sodus Point, try fishing off the inlet pier, which stretches out ¼ of a mile into Lake Ontario. Steelhead, brown, and occasionally lake trout can be taken off this concrete structure. Any time the water is free of ice is a good time to fish here.

East of Sodus come many small creeks, all hosting steelhead runs during periods of high water. Many, though, are unreachable by road, surrounded by private property or covered by heavy brush.

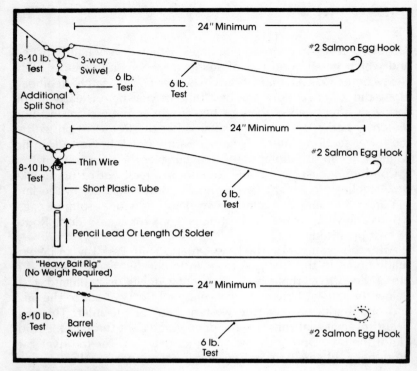

▶ *19a. STEELHEAD RIGS*

Unless you're a little masochistic, you won't find fishing them much fun, and you certainly won't take fish with any degree of consistency. Most anglers travel east to the Oswego and Little Salmon Rivers where they can find good runs of readily accessible steelhead.

Consistent steelheading is often found along the Oswego River by anglers drifting spawn bags and casting lures beneath the dam. Fish bait alongside the spillway (bring along a raincoat) or cast anywhere between the locks and the open lake.

At the Little Salmon River, if the roadway is accessible and not covered with snow, you can find fish from Little Salmon River State Park on the northern shore at the inlet or under the Route 104B bridge upstream to the first barrier.

Further north, Route 104B merges into Route 3 on its way to the Salmon River. However, just before the big river you should try Selkirk Shores State Park and the Grindstone Creek. This park and creek receive much attention. At the mouth of the creek, there's a pool which on occasion holds many steelhead and brown trout. Also, don't forget the potential of the pier and jetty found in the park where steelhead can be caught before dawn on fresh spawn bags or skein chunks fished right on the bottom or under floats.

Moving further north, you cross the Salmon River (described fully in Ch. 17) and come to Little Sandy Creek, Lindsey Creek, Skinner Creek, South Sandy Creek, and Sandy Creek. While these are all major steelhead producing waters, even during mild winters they ice over and become essentially unfishable. Still, this shouldn't stop you from planning to fish them the moment ice is out!

BAITFISHING

Over the years, more steelhead have been caught by bait fishermen using freshly wrapped bags of salmon or trout eggs than by any other means. Not only does this bait appeal to the steelhead's keen sense of sight, but it also drives their olfactory nerves crazy.

Since the vast majority of winter steelheading takes place on either the Niagara or the Salmon Rivers, let's look at some rigs that can be used with equal effectiveness at either location, but which must be used (required by law) when fishing on the Salmon River.

The first rig is imaginatively called the "Salmon River Rig" (see Fig. 18-b). It consists of a barrel swivel tied to the end of your line (10 pound test line is most effective) to which a leader (4-8 pound test preferred) of no less than 24 inches in length is attached. At the end of the leader, secure a steelhead hook using either a Palomar or Trilene knot (see Fig. 9-a). The hook itself must also conform to the law. It can't have a hook gap (the distance between shank and barb) larger than one half inch. Split-shot may be added anywhere above the barrel swivel, and bait must always be present on the hook. (Let's repeat the law: You must have a leader of no less than 24 inches in length tied to a ring or swivel at the end of your line. All weight must be above the ring or swivel. You must have a hook with no more than a ½ inch hook gap, and there must always be bait on your hook.)

Another good rig used in all steelhead waters sees the substitution of a three-way swivel for the barrel swivel. Using some very fine wire, tie a short length of rubber tubing (about an inch) to the swivel and insert either a pencil lead or length of solder coil into the tubing as weight. Then attach a leader and baited hook as described above. Should the pencil lead or solder get stuck on the bottom while you're fishing, chances are good that only the easily replaceable weight will be pulled off.

A third good rig often favored by experienced steelheaders is the "heavy bait rig." Simply tie a 24-inch leader to the barrel swivel, attach the hook and add the heavy bait. This allows you to cast a good distance and reduces snags. A "heavy bait" can be anything from a nightcrawler to a gum drop. If the current is too swift to allow the bait to get deep, light weight may be added above the swivel.

Still another rig that is very effective on steelhead is one that is often used by trout fishermen. It consists of tying a coastlock swivel to the end of your line and adding two leaders to the swivel (later called a "double leader"), one the minimum 24-inches long and the other over 30-inches. Put on bait and go to it!

PRESERVING BAIT

Since the best bait used for steelhead is either individual salmon eggs, spawn bags, or skeins, let's spend a little time right now and discuss how you can effectively prepare and preserve these baits.

To cure salmon eggs, you should carefully remove the eggs from any ripe female salmon. Store them on ice until you get home. Then, run them under cold water. Drain them for up to two hours on paper toweling, while dissolving one tablespoon of boric acid crystals in a quart of water. Then place the drained eggs into the solution. Let them remain there for up to one hour or until they lose their wrinkles and are firm to the touch. Drain and store the eggs in small airtight bottles. Refrigerate and store them for up to one year.

To make a spawn bag, ladle out a dish of fresh or preserved salmon or trout eggs. Separate enough eggs (from 4-7 eggs) to make a nickle or dime sized cluster. Place these eggs into the center of a square of white or neutral nylon mesh (an old pair of nylon stockings makes good squares) which has been cut about two inches on a side. Take up the ends and twist. Hold secure by tying rubber line or thread around the bag. Now, snip off the excess nylon and store in a small plastic vial. If possible, add some salmon egg oil to the vial to give a more fresh salmon egg smell. Tie up to 20 for a typical day.

What if you catch a female brown trout or salmon that's not

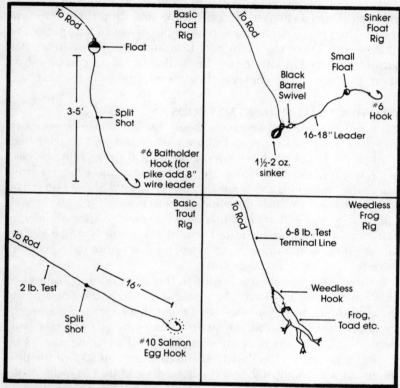

▶ **19b. RIVER FISHING RIGS**

quite ready to spawn? Instead of getting many loose eggs, you will be able to remove tightly grouped clusters of eggs. These clusters are called "skeins," and they make excellent steelhead bait. You can cut them into bag-sized clusters and fish them fresh, or you can preserve them by any of a dozen ways. I have two favorite ways to preserve skeins. With one, you first remove any excess blood from the skein and then roll and refrigerate it in paper toweling for up to three days. You then cut off bait-sized chunks and roll them in borax. Thoroughly coat the chunks with borax and store them in small, airtight bottles. You can use the skeins immediately, refrigerate for up to three weeks, or freeze.

My second preferred method is to remove the refrigerated, towel-wrapped skeins as above, cut off chunks and drop them into pure honey. Then place each chunk on an open sheet of wax paper and allow to dry. Once the skein gets firm and tight, store in a small bottle for up to a month, or use immediately. Skeins can be substituted for spawn bags wherever they are referred to in the text.

STEELHEAD BAIT FISHING METHODS

With any of these rigs and baits, begin fishing somewhere around mid-pool. Cast upstream and allow the rig and bait to drift back through the entire pool. If it's too large to drift through in one cast, begin working near the headwaters of the pool and expect a strike where the bait enters the pool. Fish this area well! Should no strikes come, move on towards the middle of the pool fishing all the way. Continue to move along and fish until you reach a spot where your bait can swing through the tail end of the pool. If no strikes are forthcoming, either move on to a new pool or return to the head of the pool and begin fishing again.

If there are other anglers fishing in the same pool, consider one location as good as another. However, if you have the opportunity, move to the head of the pool. Steelhead show a strong preference for lying in or just below the swift current where it enters a pool. Here, they like to hug the bottom and pick off anything passing by. In fact, experienced steelhead fishermen know that 90% of the time steelhead are caught right on the bottom; and that in order to get their baits near the bottom, they are going to have to get snagged a few times. Snags have, therefore, always been equated to catching fish. If you haven't been snagged at least a few times, you probably haven't been catching any fish. In light of this, here are some things you can do to minimize the snags.

Always try to use the correct amount of weight for the amount of current and distance of cast you are about to make. The further the cast or the slower the current, the less weight required. Foolish steelheaders often use the same amount of weight regardless of condition sand thereby spend much of their time hopelessly stuck to the bottom and retying broken rigs.

Another problem is that on long casts, you have less control over the weight as it drifts along in the current. If the weight's too heavy, it will immediately go to the bottom and get stuck. Play each situation as a whole new ball game and try to use only as much weight as is necessary. If there's any question about it, use less. It will be far easier to later add a little weight than to tie on an entire new rig with frozen fingers along icy banks.

Of all the above mentioned rigs, the heavy bait rig is my favorite, and the gum drop is my favorite heavy bait. Use the red, orange, yellow or green colored gum drops. Remove all the sugar from them by placing them in water or in your mouth, and then cut them into proper spawn bag sizes if necessary. Gum drops are heavy and can be cast easily without using any extra weight. They also stay on your hook remarkably well, and can be given a good scent if stored in an old salmon egg jar full of salmon egg oil.

Another good heavy bait that you may consider trying is the common nightcrawler. Steelhead and domestic rainbows alike enjoy striking nightcrawlers as they enticingly wiggle along in the current. Often these baits are unavailable during the steelhead season, so plan to bring them along with you when heading to the big lake.

Another good morsel that may be fished with weight is a single salmon egg on a small, salmon egg hook. If you have ever autopsied a steelhead's stomach, you know that you often find individual eggs in it. Give them what they are feeding on! Individual eggs can be effectively fished on fly rods with sinking fly line and 7½ to 9-foot leaders to six pound test tips; or use noodle rods with light line and with or without small split-shot for weight.

Another excellent steelhead bait is a small piece of marshmallow fished alone or in combination with a spawn bag or gum drop. The marshmallow leaves a trail of white in the water which looks very much like a skein of fertilized eggs. Make certain to frequently change the marshmallow or spawn bags, especially if they appear to have lost their scent.

Finally, try the "double leaders." Fish either spawn bags, single eggs, or heavy baits on the tandem hooks. Then watch as these baits dance down the river. With the aid of polaroid glasses, you can sometimes see interested steelhead come out of hiding and follow or strike the baits as they pass. The fish are attracted to the hypnotic motion of the baits and often take the bait right in full sight. When this occurs, strike immediately.

When fishing with weight, I often get snagged on the bottom. However, while using heavy baits, I experience very few if any snags.

CATCHING STEELHEAD ON LURES

Although bait fishermen readily catch steelhead whenever they're in the river, lure fishermen catch their fair share, too. Steelhead are usually very interested in lures presented anywhere in their vicinity. The two most commonly used lure types are floating plugs and spinners. Each of these lures is presented differently.

While fishing with floating plugs you can fish by either of two methods. The first is to simply cast across the stream and retrieve. The second is to stand in the stream and hold the lure down current in front of you and drop it back to the waiting fish.

This drop back method is best used early in the morning, when the pool in which you are fishing may contain some aggressive fish. You should enter the river about 30 feet above the pool. Allow your lure to float in the current downstream to the head of the pool. Now, engage your reel and hang on! Steelhead are very territorial. Let one think that a small fish is going to try to move it out of its position and there's big trouble. The aggravated steelhead will ferociously strike the lure at which time you may return the favor. If you do not get a strike, then move your lure around while still keeping it at the head of the pool. Make certain to cover this area thoroughly.

After a while, allow the lure to float several yards back down the pool. Engage the reel and allow the lure to work in this new section. Continue this process until the entire pool has been covered. If you know that there are steelhead in the pool (you've either seen them, or it's a pool where a few are always caught), bring your lure all the way back to the headwaters and start over again. If still nothing, move on to a new pool. This technique can be used only in pools that are void of other fishermen, because they would constantly cast over your lure and tangle your line.

It was snowing so hard you could barely see the other side of the river. Snow drifts over four feet tall were standing everywhere you looked from other storms. There was a very cold and strong wind blowing and the temperature was down near 15 degrees. I looked at Ron Jacobsen as we were about to enter the Salmon River just below the Altmar Bridge and said, "We've got to be crazy!"

Ron just smiled and continued edging his way along the bank, then began casting spawn bags across the river. Soon, I was at his side and we were both casting baits and feezing even though we were wearing thermal underwear, heavy winter clothing, and goose down jackets with hoods. Over our clothing, we had on thermal chest waders and over our hands we wore gloves inside thermal rubber gloves. Our casting glove hand had the index finger slot removed.

It soon became obvious that the steelhead weren't going to co-operate. Ron and I both began moving further downstream. After about a half an hour had passed another crazy angler wearing Neoprene waders ventured out along the opposite bank casting an illegal Tadpolly lure (on the Salmon River, you can only use float-ing lures with single treble hooks — the Tadpolly has two). On his first cast, he connected with a steelhead which jumped and threw the bright red lure.

"Can you believe that?" I called to Ron. "Here we've been using the best bait and we can't even buy a nibble! Maybe we should change?"

"Nah," he responded, "that was probably just a lucky fish."

As the unfortunate angler continued along the bank on his way toward Schoolhouse Pool, he made several more casts. On about his third attempt, he solidly connected with another big steelie.

Steelhead! One of sport fishing's most glamorous trophies makes braving the numbing weather worthwhile.

That was more than Ron could take, and he immediately turned to me and asked if I had any lures on me. I replied that I did and he suggested that I put one on.

I removed the rig I was fishing and replaced it with a sturdy ball bearing snap swivel at the end of my line. I had one Heddon Tadpolly from which I had removed the middle set of treble hooks. This made it a legal Salmon River lure, one with only one treble hook. Ron thought that he had some others back at the wagon.

As Ron made his way back up the snowy embankment, I put on the lure and made a cast across the river. The lure hadn't gotten half way back across when it stopped and the water exploded. A big steelhead had grabbed the lure and was now churning downstream! The drag screamed before the big fish tired and turned around to head back upstream toward me.

After perhaps five minutes, the spent steelhead rolled over on its side and came in towards me. I had already picked a likely spot along the bank and was able to beach the 10 pound beauty.

We had the formula, I was certain of it. But when Ron returned, we fished for close to an hour more and never received another strike. So goes the way of a February steelhead fisherman, and perhaps the way of fishermen in general. So bring lures, and bring bait, and also bring a little prayer that something will click.

DRIFTBOAT FISHING

Many anglers dream of catching just one trophy steelhead. After all, this is a beautiful fish and a tremendous fighter. Unfortunately, though, steelhead only enter rivers during the winter. During this tough time of year, when the rivers are usually very high and icy and the banks are usually waist deep with snow, the temperature never quite gets above the 20 degree mark. If you have ever wanted to catch one of these glamorous fish, but have been deterred by the weather, perhaps a steelhead driftboat trip is for you.

Most driftboat captains rent booths at boat and fishing shows around the country, and this is one way to contact them. Often, they run ads in papers and magazines, and they also put out brochures in local tackle shops. If you can't get their numbers by any of these means, try calling a local tackle shop and ask for recommendations and phone numbers. Most shops cooperate.

Let's say that you have a date and are about to leave for your first steelhead driftboat trip. You want to arrive a day ahead of time because most driftboat captains want to be on the river as early as possible. You will only have enough time to get up, eat breakfast, fill a thermos and hit the road. You won't have to worry about tackle, because all driftboat captains supply everything. However, there are a few things you can do to get ready for the six to eight hour downriver trip ahead of you.

Knowing that you will be in for a long and cold day with little chance to stand up and move around, dress accordingly. Long johns, uni-suits, felt-lined thermal boots, thermal gloves, felt-hats with ear flaps, pocket warmers, thermal seats, and plenty of hot soup or coffee is the order of the day. Remember, you will be riding high and dry, therefore you need not pack chest waders (unless you intend to fish an extra day on your own).

Remember to have an alarm clock — often motels have a few spares around. Set the alarm early, have your breakfast but try to leave some extra time between eating and your departure time. When your captain arrives at the motel or restaurant, he will want to immediately head for the river.

He will have you follow him in your car and park at a location where the driftboat trip will end. At this time, you should remember to grab anything from your car that you may want — cameras, a thermos, a lure you may want to try, etc. From where you park (usually the Compactor Pool on the Salmon River) to where you put the boat into the river (at the Altmar Bridge on the Salmon) is about a 12 minute drive, which you'll run up in the captain's car.

Once at the bridge, your guide will get everything set up and park his car. You and a companion (2 man trips) will get seated in the front of the boat and the captain will shove off. It's that quick! Under the Altmar Bridge and you're off on your first steelhead adventure down the winding Salmon River.

The moment you get beyond the bridge, you and your partner will pick up the rods with reels full of from 14-17 pound test line. On the end of the line will be a lure. Let out about eight complete turns of the levelwind reel and your lure should be about 35 feet downstream of the boat.

As you are doing this, the captain will begin steadily rowing against the current. He will not try to row upstream as much as just try to stop the boat, or allow the boat to move ever so slowly downstream. However, he will be rowing enough to cause the lures to work. With the lures working, the captain will drift them into position at the head of each pool and through every pool all the way down the river.

One problem that usually crops up right around now is what to do with the third rod? How we usually handle this is to toss a coin. The winner gets to hold the third rod, and he keeps holding it until he goes ahead in numbers of fish caught (some prefer number of strikes). Sometimes lucky anglers never get to fish the two rods!

ADRIFT ON THE BEAUTIFUL SALMON

One Salmon River trip I took will serve to make some examples and to further acquaint you with the river.

Soon after passing under the Altmar Bridge, we entered School-house Pool. The sun hadn't even risen, yet there were some 20 die hards lined up along the bank and preparing to fish. It was there that Joe caught his first fish of the day.

"Keep the rods pointed ahead," said captain Ron Clark. "The moment a fish strikes, lift straight up on it hard."

Joe Rosa looked at me and said, "If anything's going to happen, I hope it happens soon. I'm frozen!"

No sooner did he get those words out of his mouth when Ron yelled, "the left rod, pull! pull!"

Joe was holding the rod and pulled to Ron's command. As he yanked the big rod about a third of the way up, it curled right back down again. This time Joe really layed it to the fish, pulling the nine-foot Ugly Stik all the way up. The rod remained doubled over.

"Now you can see why we point the rods at the lure. That way we can really set the hook," Ron pointed out.

Well, Joe eventually boated the first and then the second fish of the day. Later I managed to catch the third and fifth, but Joe was ahead all the time and don't think I ever lived down holding both those rods all day.

From the Schoolhouse Pool, we slowly drifted downstream with Captain Ron Clark rowing with all his might against the current. "What a great way to learn about the river's pools," I can remember saying as we rounded a bend and headed west for the Trestle Pool.

Since there were many people fishing at the Trestle, Ron decided to sail on. Soon, he stopped the boat with an anchor. There, we practiced the "drop back" technique into the next pool, while Ron regathered his strength. After a quick cup of coffee, off we went again.

As we approached Sheepskin Road, Joe caught his second steelhead. This one tipped the scales at eight pounds, and was just slightly larger than his first.

Soon after boating the fish, we were on our way again. Going under the Pineville Bridge, my rod was struck. The fish ran off to the side and Ron yelled, "that's a big fish!"

Well, that fish fought for close to 10 minutes. First he got close to the boat and then he'd pull away. Right...left...and once around the boat. Finally he lined up directly off our bow and ever so slowly gave way to the pressure of the rod. Ron placed the big net under the fish and soon we had a beautiful, prize, steelhead quaking on the bottom of the boat.

Although I've caught thousands of fish, that 13-pound steelhead left me shaking for 20 minutes. It's line-stripping runs were simply dazzling. It must have taken 30 minutes all together to calm down and get back into the routine of just being cold.

Below Pineville, we floated through the Sportsman's Pool. This pool is about a quarter of a mile from any road. But in spite of the deep snow, the ice, the cold, and the still very early hour of the morning, we counted 35 people fishing along the Route 13 side of the pool and another 22 on the Centerville Road side. Fifty-seven fishermen in one very large pool!

After shooting the rapids beneath Sportsman's Pool, Ron rowed the boat over to the side where he made a small fire and cooked us some hotdogs. We all had something warm to drink and moved around trying to regain some of the feeling we had lost while sitting for so long in the boat.

After eating, Ron promised us that we'd be floating through three more good pools. Back into the boat we climbed and eventually we nailed another fish apiece before pulling the boat out of the river back at Compactor Pool where we had left our car.

"Two o'clock," Ron said, "that's about right." Our trip had taken in the neighborhood of seven hours. We had nine good strikes and we boated five fish.

If you want to get in on this action, remember that steelhead driftboating takes place during two distinct seasons. The first begins around November and lasts until mid-December. Then, it stops for awhile during the very cold winter (fishermen still use the banks all winter long). The "second season" begins again late in February and lasts until early April.

Steelhead make great mounts. They are very long and slender fish. The 13-pounder we caught that day taped out at 31 inches. Would you like to have something like that across your mantle? If so, remember to always point your rods at the working lures, strike with all your might, and don't fret if you lose the coin toss and only get to hold one rod.

ENJOYING YOUR CATCH

PART IV

PRELIMINARY CARE AND PREPARATION

"Follow these simple and easy steps... when you get back that beautiful mount, you'll know that this extra effort was worth it."

20

The fish you intend to keep should be cared for immediately. A large ice chest (75-151 quart) is necessary to handle fish up to 20 pounds. By placing the freshly caught fish on ice, you will preserve their good, firm meat. If not placed on ice, the fish will quickly begin to deteriorate. This is most critical with salmon caught in the river, since they are already deteriorating when they enter the river. Any hesitation here only compounds the matter (it should be noted that the longer a ready-to-spawn salmon remains in the tributary, the poorer eating condition it will be in).

If you're in a boat catching trout or salmon, try to kill them before placing them on ice. If the fish are allowed to thrash around in a cooler or fish well they will only succeed in bruising their own flesh. One sharp "klunk" on the head is all that's required. As more fish are added to the box, the bruise potential is decreased.

On charters or guided river excursions, expect your fish to be cleaned as part of the deal — no extra cost, but perhaps a tip. Most captains or guides will go out of their way to clean the fish exactly the way you want them. Since there are fish cleaning alternatives — gutting, filleting, steaking, etc. — read this and the next chapter before planning on how to cut and package your fish.

DRESSING YOUR CATCH

Immediately upon getting back to a fish cleaning station, wash the fish and remove scales with a fish scraper. Scales scatter, so try to do this in the yard or somewhere out in the open. Cut to the back bone just behind the head and break the head loose. Cut through the remainder of the fish and discard the head. Next, place knife in the anal vent and, cutting the belly skin, bring forward to where the head was removed. Remove all entrails. Run a fingernail or knife along backbone in body cavity to remove all congealed blood. Remove the dorsal (upper back) fin by cutting around it and gently pulling it free of the fish. Remove the caudal (tail) fin by cutting across the meaty section just before it. Now, the fish can be pan fried (if it's small), cut into steaks or even filleted.

If your stay is going to be more than a day or two, freeze your catch into a solid block. Ice houses, local grocery stores, and tackle shops often rent anglers freezer space. The fee can be a nominal $1.50 per day per large fish. Some motels and guest houses allow you to use their freezers at no cost. Fish stored in this manner should last several months.

Big fish need big coolers. A good size is 100-qts., but 150 won't hurt.

If your stay will be shorter, clean or fillet your fish, wrap them in freezer paper and store them in plastic bags on ice. Be careful not to freeze any fish that may defrost on your trip home, as refreezing is taboo. It is far better to keep the cleaned fish on ice for a day or more and only freeze upon returning home.

If you are fishing a stream, the water will usually be quite cool so you can keep your fish on a stringer (see below) in clean running water that is well shaded. If this isn't possible, simply place the fish on the ground out of direct sunlight, but try to keep the ground around them wet. As the water evaporates, it will tend to cool the fish. If the weather is still quite cool, these simple precautions will suffice.

Salmon fishermen should make certain to bring along with them streamside a good strong length of rope, preferably nylon. Imagine catching three nice chinook salmon, perhaps a 37 pounder, another of 34 pounds and a third one that's about 26 pounds. Great catch, but how are you going to get them back to the car? That's 97 pounds total! With a rope, you can float the fish along with you as you move through the water and when you leave the water, you can drag them to your car. This may slightly bruise the fish, but it may also prevent a hernia.

FISH CARCASS DISPOSAL LAW

Remember that, with certain exceptions, it is illegal to discard any fish carcass, or parts thereof (entrails) into the freshwaters of the state. The best way to cooperate with this law is to bring your catch to a fish cleaning station, located behind most tackle shops. Here, someone will clean your fish for a fee. With the salmon the fee is usually the eggs. Also, along the Salmon River, many enterprising families have set up parking facilities and fish cleaning stations. Each has a different fee, but well worth whatever it might be. They dispose of the carcasses, and you get your cleaned fish.

You may elect to field dress your catch or fillet it streamside. This is allowed only if you do not discard the carcass or carcass parts. Make sure you bring along several plastic bags to carry both the fillets and carcasses, the latter to be disposed of in the proper place.

Trout are tender fish and should be handled gently. Try to keep them alive after being caught for as long as possible. When fishing a river, it is best to place your trout on a stringer lodged in fast moving, clean water. The motion of the water will keep the fish well oxygenated and calm. However, keep an eye on them, because they will make a very tempting treat for any passing otter, mink, or weasel!

When fishing for smaller varieties of stream trout that do not run the big lake, you should use a wicker creel. Canvas creels, especially with plastic inserts, should be avoided. These creels often bake the fish before you can get them back to your car. For best results, line your creel with wet leaves. Don't use grass! Leaves will keep your catch wet and help soak up any excess slime,while the grass will only discolor your fish and make them harder to clean.

Remember to keep your creel cool. In fact, a cool dip in water every now and then can't hurt. Also, keep it out of direct sunlight. At the end of the day, wash the creel thoroughly. This will help guarantee that no flies or other insects will lay eggs on its surface. Never leave trout in a creel overnight.

For carrying big fish, like pike, salmon, or muskies, maintain a cooler in the car with ice or better yet, dry ice. Then, once you return to your lodging look into deep freezing your catch. Also, remember not to feeze more fish than you can legally carry in New York State. No more than a two day's legal take of non-salable fish may be transported unless a permit is obtained first from a DEC Regional Office.

▶ *Rich Giessuebel with some of his impressive Lake Ontario trophies.*

CARE FOR TROPHIES TO BE MOUNTED

If you intend to mount a fish, be extra careful with it. The best thing you can do is kill it quickly with a sharp blow to the head. This usually stuns the fish and quickly stops him from flopping around. You may feel that you can damage the head by doing this, but many taxidermists discard the top portion of the head anyway. This is because it is the oiliest section of the entire fish. Next, wrap the fish in a wet towel. Then run several strips of tape around the towel.

If you follow these simple and easy steps, you will succeed in keeping all the fins intact and the fish will not be able to scar or bruise itself. Also, if you can take a picture of the fish before you wrap it up, the taxidermist will be able to replicate its colors. When you get back that beautiful mount you'll know that this extra effort was worth it.

If you are on a boat, do the same thing with any fish that has the earmarkings of a wall fish. Make certain not to clean or have cleaned the intended fish by a mate after you've returned to the dock. Separate the fish to be mounted from the fish to be cleaned. Then, wrap the former neatly in a towel, moisten it and place it on ice. Later, freeze the entire bundle — fish, towel, and all! Since you do not intend to eat this fish, it doesn't matter if it is frozen, thawed and then refrozen.

Let's try to summarize some of the important points made in this chapter and add a few more simple "Do's and Don'ts" for fish handling:

Do's! Do gut, gill, and ice fish as soon as possible. Do wash the gutted fish in lake water, creek water, saltwater, or tap water to remove as much slime, mud, and blood as possible before icing. Do wrap fish in damp paper or cloth and store in a shady, well ventilated area if ice is unavailable. This will keep the flesh moist and cool. Do allow for proper bleeding by cutting off either the head or tail and positioning the fish in an ice chest so as to drain the blood out thoroughly. Blood remaining in the tissue can increase rancidity that develops in fish in frozen storage. Do ice the fish generously before transporting them home. Pack the belly cavity with ice and provide adequate ice between fish and also between any fish and the sides of the cooler. Make a false bottom in your chest so that your fish will not be floating in bloody, melted ice water when you get home.

Don'ts! Don't let a fish flop around in the bottom of a boat or on a pier. This will bruise the flesh and speed up biochemical changes (rigor mortis) that may produce an undesirable taste. Don't keep fish on a crowded stringer in shallow, muddy, and warm water. Don't leave the gills and guts in a fish for very long after the fish has died. Most marinas, fishing piers, state parks, etc. have facilities for cleaning fish, and unless you have adequate space at home, it is probably best to make use of the facilities.

Finally, if you intend to transport these fish home with you by air, make certain that your cooler is packed with dry ice, is perfectly sealed, has no leaks, and is tied with strong cord to preclude the possibility of it turning upside down, opening, and spilling the fish out all over the place. If you follow these precautions, most airlines will allow you to take your fish along with you. However, it's still best to ask the airline you're flying how you should bundle your catch for the flight back home. Rules will vary.

FAVORITE REGIONAL RECIPES

"With Norwegian Salmon around $16 the pound and Pacific Salmon often up over $20, a 30-pound chinook is not a prize to be taken lightly."

▼

21

In this chapter we'll pick up where we left off in Ch. 20 on the subject of preparing your catch for consumption. Some of the procedures we discuss here may continue at streamside (or lakeside) though some may be carried out in the backyard, basement or kitchen.

Before we go further, an important topic should be addressed, and that is the size of the fish. Not too many east coast anglers are accustomed to dragging home 20 pound and better fresh water fish! What implications, it any, does that have for the chef?

Treatment of these bruisers may be quite similar to that given small fish. For one thing, you'll get nice thick, clean fillets, and most diners do prefer fish without bones. But unlike a smaller fish, you may not need or want to broil (or otherwise render) the entire fillet. Cut only as much off it as you need then cook it as you would a whole fillet from a smaller fish. Since the fillet (or piece thereof) may be thicker, cook longer. A good broiling rule of thumb is 10 minutes per inch of thickness. This applies to all fish.

Another way to prepare a fish for cooking is steaking. You may not have done this too often because it doesn't work too well with smaller fish. But from those big Ontario trout and salmon, especially those over 10 pounds, steaks look nice and they hold together well. It's a method you might want to try and we'll tell you exactly how.

Pan frying is always popular, and you can certainly do a tasty sauté with the panfish and smaller stream trout you take from Ontario and its tributaries. Yellow perch, in particular, are delicious when filleted and fried. We'll give you a filleting tip or two and a good frying recipe.

Perhaps the most noteworthy culinary treat yielded by Ontario is the salmon. With Norwegian Salmon often up around $16 the pound, and imported Pacific Salmon almost always above $20, a thirty pound chinook is not a prize to be taken lightly! Salmon is one of the finest eating fish in the world, and so we've given it a separate little section in this chapter.

Pickerel, pike and muskellunge are long, thin, hard fighting — and bony. But we'll give you a recipe that will literally dissolve all those small bones. It's an appetizing appetizer that goes perfectly with a before dinner cocktail.

Last but not least, we'll give you a fine recipe for smelt, one of the finest eating fish in the world.

STEAKING YOUR CATCH

This technique is best done on fish weighing over eight pounds. After completely dressing your catch (see Ch. 20), lay the fish belly down on a solid wood cutting board. Using a serrated knife (a sharp steak or bread knife will make a good choice) cut across the back of the fish making sections that are betwen 1 and 1½ inches thick. Continue cutting all along the fish until you reach the posterior dorsal fin. Most do not cut any further; what's left will be one good-sized section that extends to where the tail begins.

FILLETING YOUR CATCH

Although you can fillet a fish that has been gutted, the filleting process works best on fish that have not been dressed. With the fish laying flat on its side, and using a sharp 3-5 inch thin-bladed knife, make an incision beginning in the back of the fish just behind its head. Run the knife under the skin for the full length of the fish all along its back. Make certain to pass on the upper side of all fins. Now, get a hold of the skin and meat near the beginning of the incision and pull slightly apart. With the knife, continue to cut the meat away from the body cage from the head to just below the dorsal fin. Then, run the knife through the fish at this point and take the meat off to the tail. Go back and continue to work on the fore section until you reach the belly. Now, cut through the skin in this area and remove the fillet. To de-skin, hold the skin firmly by the end nearest the tail. Slice the knife through the meat about an inch in front of your grip. Now, pull the skin out allowing the knife (which you do not have to move) to strip the meat from it. Turn the fish over and repeat the process.

Once the fillets have been removed, wash them thoroughly, then dry on paper towels. Remove any remaining scales and bones. If you are not going to eat the fillets immediately, wrap them in freezer paper or wax paper and then in plastic bags.

SMOKING FISH

Before smoking, the fish is placed in a salt (brine) solution which helps preserve them for much longer periods of time. Here are two brine formulas. The first brine is made by adding 1½ cups of kosher salt to one gallon of cold water. Marinate the fish in it for at least 14 hours in a refrigerator at 40 degrees. The second is made by adding 3½ cups of salt to one gallon of cold water. In this solution, the fish need only be marinated for 30 minutes at 40 degrees. Drain, rinse, and place the fish into your smoker. Spread wet wood chips — hickory, beech, white birch or ash — on the heater unit or charcoal to produce smoke. Smoke for up to eight hours, or until the internal temperature of the fish is at 250 degrees for 30 minutes. Remove the fish from the smoker and refrigerate. It will keep for a month or sometimes longer.

Small whole fish or fillets, or chunks of larger fish, can be pan fried with excellent results. Use part butter and part oil. The butter is for flavor, the oil is to help prevent burning.

Yellow perch are both abundant and very much appreciated in the Ontario region. Fillet them just like a trout or other round fish but don't worry too much about the part of the fish *below* the center (horizontal) line. Just take the nice thick fillet from the top (dorsal fin) down to the center. Only on the largest perch will you be able to take a clean piece off those abdominal bones.

PERFECT PERCH

5-6 yellow perch, skinned and
  filleted
1 egg
Flavored bread crumbs

2 tbsp. oil or more
2 tbsp. butter
Flour

Wash the fillets and pat dry. Dredge in flour. Dip in egg, then in bread crumbs. Place on a wire rack for 15 minutes to set the coating. Sauté in a mixture of butter and oil, about 5 minutes a side.

SAUTEED TROUT (serves 4)

4 whole small trout (same size)
¼ cup flour
7 tbsp. butter, divided
¼ cup oil, preferably peanut oil

Salt & fresh ground pepper
  to taste
1 tbsp. minced parsley
Lemon wedges

Coat fish lightly with flour, shaking off excess. Heat 4 tbsp. butter and oil in large heavy skillet. When hot but not smoking, add fish and cook over med-high heat half the estimated cooking time, seasoning with salt and pepper. Turn and cook remaining half of time or until fish flakes easily when tested with fork. Remove to hot platter. Melt remaining 3 tbsp. butter in skillet, stir in parsley and pour over fish. Serve at once with lemon wedges.

TROUT IN WHITE WINE (serves 2)

Salt & pepper   1 cup heavy cream
1 lemon   1 lb. trout
1 tsp. butter
½ cup white wine (or Champagne)

Season trout with salt and pepper. Place in buttered casserole dish and sprinkle juice of one lemon and ½ cup of white wine (or Champagne) over trout. Cover and bake in moderate oven at 350° for 15 minutes. Pour ½ cup of heavy cream over fish and place under broiler until sauce is brown. Keep broiler door open and watch carefully. Serve hot.

BEER BATTER BASS (serves 10)

Fresh fillets (8-10 lbs.)   3 12-oz. bottles beer
1½ tbsp. lemon juice   ¼ cup paprika
2 tsp. salt   1 cup water
1 qt. flour   Oil

Cut fillets into serving sized pieces. Sprinkle fillets with lemon juice and salt. Combine flour and paprika and gradually stir in water and beer until batter is smooth. Coat fish and fry in hot deep oil until browned (4-5 minutes). Drain on paper towels and serve with tartar sauce.

PANFISH PATTY BURGERS (serves 6)

1½ lbs. panfish fillets   3 beaten eggs
1 qt. boiling water   1/3 cup grated parmesan cheese
1 tbsp. salt   1 tbsp. chopped parsley
Dash of pepper   6 burger rolls
1 finely chopped garlic clove   ½ cup dry bread crumbs

Place 1½ lbs. of panfish (perch preferred) fillets into salted water. Bring to a boil, simmer for 6-8 minutes or until fish becomes flaky. Remove fillets. Mix fish, 3 beaten eggs, parsley, garlic, cheese, salt and pepper and chill. Make 6 patties and coat with bread crumbs. Fry each side until brown. Drain on paper towels. Place in roll and add catsup, tartar sauce, or a mixture of mayonnaise and catsup to taste.

CAPPY'S LIME MARINATED TROUT (serves 3)

1 lb. trout fillets, not too thick
(preferably about 5 pieces)
¼ cup fresh lime juice
Salt and pepper

Tarragon or dill, preferably fresh
Onion powder
Butter for basting

Marinate the fillets in lime juice at room temperature for 1 hour, turning a few times. Pre-heat the broiler, and grease. Place fillets on broiler rack. Chop tarragon or dill and mix with melted butter. Brush this on the fillets along with a little onion powder. Broil about 10 minutes per inch of thickness. Do not turn if fillets are very thin.

SUPER BAKED FISH À LA ANN (serves 1-2)

2 clean fillets from white
fleshed fish
3 tbsp. mayonnaise
Unflavored bread crumbs

1 tbsp. lemon juice
¼ tsp. onion salt
Paprika

Butter a baking dish. Put in fillets. Mix salt, juice and mayonnaise and spread on fish. Sprinkle on crumbs and paprika. Optional: Sprinkle on some minced, dry onion. Bake at 400° for 20 minutes, less if fillets are thin.

Salmon are among the most flavorful and highly prized of all fish. Often, salmon is simply poached and then knapped with a sauce like Hollandaise. But the possibilities are really endless.

SURFSIDE SALMON

1 slice lemon
1 slice onion
1 bay leaf
1 tsp. pepper
½ tsp. salt for salmon
Few celery leaves
2 lbs. salmon steaks

1½ tsp. butter
1½ tbsp. flour
1 cup fish stock
½ tsp. salt for sauce
¼ cup green pepper, minced

Fill a large skillet half full of water. Add lemon, onion, bay leaf, ½ tsp. of pepper, ½ tsp. salt and celery leaves. Bring to a boil.

Put in the salmon. Simmer for fifteen minutes. While the fish cooks, make a sauce by melting butter and blending in flour to make a smooth paste. Add one cup of liquid from the fish and stir constantly until thick and smooth. Add diced celery, green pepper and a half teaspoon of salt. Cook for five minutes. When the fish is done, remove to a platter and cover with sauce.

SALMON IN RED WINE SAUCE (serves 2)

4 oz. red wine
2 tbsp. sliced shallots
½ bay leaf
1 parsley sprig

⅛ tsp. thyme
2 salmon steaks (8 oz. each)
2 tsp. margarine
1 tbsp. chopped parsley

In a small saucepan bring wine, shallots, bay leaf, parsley sprig and thyme to a boil. Reduce heat; cover and simmer 20 minutes. Strain; discard solids. Return liquid to saucepan, set aside. Place salmon in single layer in non-stick baking pan just large enough to fit snugly. Spoon 1 tbsp. wine sauce over each steak. Cover; bake in preheated oven at 375° F. for 15 minutes or until flaky.

TARTAR SAUCE

1 cup mayonnaise
3 tbsp. finely chopped onion
3 tbsp. finely chopped sweet
   pickles

3 tbsp. parsley
3 tbsp. finely chopped stuffed
   olives

Mix all ingredients together, chill and serve.

Pike and pickerel and the much less commonly caught muskellunge are known for being boney. But they are also known for having very clean, tasty white flesh. First, you have to know how to fillet these fish to remove as many of their small bones as possible. Have someone show you if possible. Then, there will still be some small abdominal bones remaining. The following recipe actually pickles the fish and dissolves any small bones that your knife misses.

KATE RUTHERFORD'S PICKLED PICKEREL (makes many appetizers)

Fillet and cut into bite-sized chunks 2-3 lbs. of pickerel or pike. Layer generously with salt and cover with cold water for 24 hours (this firms the flesh). De-salt thoroughly by soaking and rinsing with cold water until rinse water no longer tastes salty. Mix the well-drained fish with cooled brine and refrigerate. It will be ready to eat in 3-5 days; bones will all be dissolved in 1 week.

Brine: Boil the following together for 10 minutes.

1 cup water
1 cup white vinegar
1 cup white wine
¼ cup sugar

3 minced cloves garlic
2 tbsp. whole mixed pickling spices, from which all cloves are removed

Add coarsely sliced onions and boil 5 minutes longer. (Be sure to cool brine before adding fish.)

BAKED NORTHERN PIKE SUPREME (serves 6)

2 lbs. northern pike fillets
1½ tsp. salt
¼ cup chopped onion
2 tbsp. melted fat or oil
1 cup chopped parsley
2 cans (4 oz. each) drained sliced mushrooms

1 tbsp. lemon juice
1½ cups soft bread crumbs
6 slices tomato
¼ cup grated cheese

Cut fillets into 6 serving size portions. Sprinkle with salt and pepper. Place single layer in well-greased baking pan. Cook mushrooms and onion in fat until tender and add parsley. Combine egg and lemon juice. Brush fish with egg mixture and top with bread crumbs. Spread mushroom mixture over tomatoes and sprinkle with cheese. Bake in moderate oven at 350° F. for 30-35 minutes or until fish is flaky.

WHOLE STUFFED SMELTS (serves 6)

2 doz. smelts
2 tbsp. lemon juice
2 doz. anchovy fillets
¼ cup melted butter or margarine

½ cup white wine
salt & pepper
2 tbsp. fine dry bread crumbs

Heat oven to 375° F. (moderate). Split smelts lengthwise and remove bones. Brush each fish with lemon juice. Place an anchovy fillet on each smelt and roll. Secure with toothpicks. Place on shallow greased baking pan. Drizzle with butter and wine. Sprinkle with salt, pepper and bread crumbs. Bake uncovered at 375° F. for 25-30 minutes or until the smelts are tender.